HANDYMAN of the LORD

HANDYMAN of the LORD

The Life and Ministry of the Rev. William Holmes Borders

by

JAMES W. ENGLISH

MEREDITH PRESS
New York

First edition

Library of Congress Catalog Card Number: 67-12637

MANUFACTURED IN THE UNITED STATES OF AMERICA FOR MEREDITH PRESS

This book is dedicated to
Julia Pate Borders
(1907–1965)
by her loving husband,
William Holmes Borders

Preface

As EACH LONG hot summer brings new street riots and civil rights marches, more and more Americans shed their apathetic views toward the so-called Negro problem. If nothing else, the intimacy of the television screen has brought the riots into their own homes. The intrusion of this violence into their private lives has caused sharp reactions. They might claim that insufficient knowledge of the Vietnam situation prevents their forming an opinion about that, but the same logic does not apply to the problem in the Negro ghetto. Those old bromides and calumnies, which have shadowed the Negro these one hundred years since his emancipation, became substitutes for truth and knowledge. The rash of opinions offered are not solutions to a problem but reactions against it.

This book offers no solution to the racial problem, other than to press for more personal understanding between the races. It is difficult for me to solve a problem until I understand it. In my business, to sell a person, I must understand him and his needs. Then, in a climate of mutual confidence and respect, we reach agreements. This has been my approach to the problem of selling to the Negro churches of America. After a slow start I have enjoyed modest success, have delighted in the experience, a fact my Negro friends quickly sensed.

Out of my personal experiences, out of observation and continuous contact, I have accumulated a positive view of the Negro community. Yes, there are deep problems, but there is also strong and capable leadership. Feeling this way, I react sharply to the negative opinions so often expressed. I counter each negative point with a positive example from my personal experience. Probably I am a bore, but generally I am listened to. After all, success stories in the Negro ghetto are rare in our media of mass communication. Thus, in a very real sense, I became aware of establishing a communications bridge across a gulf which separates most Negro and white Americans.

This book is one of those positive stories. It is intended as a communications bridge, not a structured biography, although it is shaped entirely around one man's life. It is the story of his struggle out of poverty, of his fight for education, of his steadfast efforts to meet the needs of his people. I hope it pictures him as he is, warm, friendly, possessed of a wonderful sense of humor. I have tried to set forth his many, and I think remarkable, accomplishments for his people, for his home community of Atlanta. All Americans, I think, can take pride in his efforts to eliminate a sickness in our society. I am proud to know him as a friend.

The Reverend William Holmes Borders and I had hoped this book would be published before the death of his beloved wife. This was not possible. Therefore I asked him to write a dedication to Mrs. Borders, who played a significant role in that leadership which made possible the Wheat Street story in Atlanta, Georgia.

Dundee, Illinois J. W. E.

Contents

	Preface	vii
1	Homecoming	3
2	All Uphill	18
3	The Tests	36
4	Real Religion	48
5	Civil Rights	62
6	The Lord's Business	72
7	The Bus Strike	88
8	Failure	100
9	Progress	110
10	Teamwork	127
11	Housing	143
12	After the Marches	152
13	A Long, Long Way	162

HANDYMAN of the LORD

1

Homecoming

THE BIG BLACK SEDAN had crowded the speed limit all the way from Atlanta. Just outside Macon, Georgia, the car turned down a dusty country lane and came to a complete halt on the crest of a small hill. The road continued down gentle slopes to a creek in a hollow. Beside the creek stood a little church, its weatherworn wooden slabs and squat bell tower partially screened by the scraggly green boughs of some hickory trees.

The driver, an immaculately dressed man of middle years, looked at the scene with the eyes of one who had been there before. As the seventh child of the Reverend James Buchanan Borders, once pastor of this Swift Creek Baptist Church, he had worked long hours with his parents to sweat and grind out the family's livelihood.

On those Sunday mornings long ago, he had stopped on the hilltop as he drove a wagon loaded with ice for the church dinners. The two one-hundred-pound cakes of ice were to cool lemonade for the bountiful meal that always followed his father's preaching service. Long before anyone else in the household was awake, he would have arisen, hitched up the mule, and driven the six miles to Macon, rain or shine. He had never complained, for he loved those Sunday dinners. Food had never been plentiful in his father's house, and he had always eagerly looked forward to the variety of tasty foods served from the covered dishes at these church dinners.

His daddy saw these dinners as evidence of Christian fellowship, the building of Christian character, and the strengthening of Christian faith. To young Holmes—he answered to his middle name for there was a previous William among the family's eight children—these dinners, with their spicy dressings and rich gravies, were proof that he would have a full stomach when he fell asleep that night.

The old mule had always stopped at the crest of this hill unless the driver's foot was pressed against the wagon's wheel brake. For several miles the mule had probably done the steering, while he napped. The sudden halt of the wagon's swaying motion had always awakened him, but this was not the way he now remembered the event. Memory told him he had been awakened by the voices of the congregation, reaching out to him on this hill as they sang the morning's first hymn.

The singing was a cappella for the little church could afford neither organ nor piano. This had left the congregation dependent upon his mother's clear voice to establish the pitch and set the short or long meter beat of the rhythm.

He recalled how his daddy would introduce a hymn.

"Now we goin' to sing 'Jesus the Light of the World.' "

Then his daddy would turn to his mother and say, "Now you take us up to heaven, not over to the cemetery."

On this hilltop the congregation's soft, loving, worshipful voice had reached him as through stereophonic sound.

We walk in the light, beautiful light.
It shines all around us by day and by night.

If the singing was harmonious and inspiring, his daddy's powerful voice would boom forth.

"Friends, you're singing for God. Make the angels happy. Raise up another chorus."

In this church, in the year 1913, when he had been just a lad of eight, the Lord had found him and told him to be a preacher like his daddy. This had been no dramatic confrontation, no Damascus Road experience. Instead, in a little boy's joyful heart there grew the realization that the Lord could use another handyman, even him, William Holmes Borders.

The pure emotional faith of these recalled childhood experiences brought to mind a more recent experience. A white man and wife, obviously surprised to discover the Negro couple enjoying the same round-the-world tour were an Atlanta preacher and his wife, said rather wistfully, "Most of us get very sick of our sophistication. We wish we had some of the religious fervor of your deep faith. It is so much a part of you."

Indeed, he had been lucky. God had given him parents possessed of religious fervor, who firmly believed in God, and who prayed regularly and meaningfully with their children. All his life the Reverend Mr. Borders had tried to spend one hour each day in prayer with God. Now that he was pastor to the five thousand members of the Wheat Street Baptist Church in Atlanta, it was sometimes difficult to take a full hour alone with the Master; so he had come back to this little church, where the Lord had first called him, to pray. His problem was a century old. It dealt with the fears and frustrations of his people yet in search of freedom's elusive promise.

This was in the mid-1950's and the civil rights voices were many and varied, and not always in harmony as to the best methods and timing to be followed. Confronted by this confusion of programs, each supported by the honest entreaties of fellow ministers, he had felt more than ever the need of God's guidance through prayer.

To a stranger the inside of the little church was as barren as the outside, but Borders saw the sanctuary with the loving eye of one returned home. Out of habit from years past, he tiptoed down the one aisle, and in front of the pulpit lectern slid into a timeworn and oft scrubbed front bench. Years before, after the ice had been delivered to the church kitchen, he always sat on this front seat and listened to his daddy preach one of his fiery gospel messages.

Although today he had come to pray, Borders first sat still amid a surge of memories. Most thoughts were of his parents, but he did recall one visiting preacher, old in years and bent of body, whose direct prayer petition he had recently retold in a short book of published poems.

Lord, this little William talking to you,
You know me better than I know myself, and I know you.
But I want to be sure I got the *main line* . . .

Today Borders felt this same way. He had driven home to Swift Creek Baptist Church to be sure his prayer got on the main line.

. . . Thank you for giving up the third
part of yourself as our overseer,
So that we can rub up against our boss man.

Many times his heart had been quickened by the presence of the Holy Spirit in this sanctuary, and he had confidence now that his prayer needs would be answered if he proved deserving.

His earliest recollection was of riding in a buggy to this

church with his father. All the way his daddy talked about a powerful, rewarding, and all-knowing person called God.

His mother had been a saintly Christian woman. When it stormed, the family huddled together in the hall. They sat shoulder to shoulder while the thunder muttered, the lightning flashed, and his mother prayed or sang her favorite hymn, "I'm a Child of the King." When it stormed, his mother believed God was hard at work. In her reverence for him there were elements of fear, awe, and fascination.

Theirs had been an extremely poor family. His mother canned foods and sewed for some white families to supplement his father's monthly forty-dollar salary. However, if it rained on the preacher's Sunday—the day the entire month's salary was supposed to be given in the church collection, his daddy's take-home pay was often short of the allowable and promised amount.

His parents told him it had rained on the night of his birth, rained right onto the bed where he was being delivered. He had been born in the best room of their four-room house. The other rooms were almost untenable when it rained.

His mother died at the age of fifty. He had been twelve at the time. Six months later an older sister married and left home. For the rest of the family there were difficult days ahead. This period marked the start of his father's physical downfall. Farm families had started moving to the cities, and the elder Borders faced increasing problems in this little rural church. However, the problem at home was constant. It was impossible for this harried man to make both ends meet as he tried to provide for his family of eight on his preacher's income. Finally he mortgaged their home.

The son's present memories, however, were not so much of past wants and needs as of his father, standing firm like an oak in this same pulpit as he preached a Bible message.

His daddy had been an imposing figure of a man, standing just under six feet and weighing nearly two hundred pounds. He was half Cherokee and half Negro and one did not easily forget his countenance. There were piercing dark eyes which he could roll until only their clear whites showed. His ready laugh revealed a perfect set of flashing white teeth. The Indian ancestry gave his skin a clear coppery tone. But the most distinctive part of his physical appearance was his long and absolutely straight white hair.

The son chuckled. His daddy's greatest vanity was that long, straight white hair. When down at the creek baptizing, the elder Borders never waded into the water without first slipping a hairbrush into his back pocket. When finished with the baptisms, he would take the hairbrush from his pocket and carefully brush each strand of that straight white hair into place before emerging from the water.

His father's pulpit delivery had been dramatic. Restlessly, he would pace the rostrum from one side to the other. His voice was marvelously controlled. Without speech training, he had learned to project his booming voice in fully managed tones, or to modulate it into a mere whisper that nevertheless carried to the farthest corners of the sanctuary.

A marvelous storyteller, his father knew how to take a Bible story and in its telling stand a congregation on its head. Thus his sermons became a testament of biblical record and the personal witness of his deep and childlike faith in God. He illustrated each biblical truth by clothing it in a down-to-earth translation of the classic English of the King James Bible. For instance, when describing Jesus feeding the multitude, his daddy said, "Jesus took a little boy's sack lunch and opened a fish market and a bakery shop."

Through the easily understood metaphor of the uneducated, his daddy had spoken fluently to his congregation. He had sought to force them out of their wallow of self-pity into realization that they too were children of God and expected to carry his Cross.

The son had never once heard his father criticize anyone by name. If unable to speak well of a person, his daddy remained silent. Yet if a personal reprimand was needed, he always found a rural truism to apply to the situation. One of his father's favorite barnyard barbs had been, "The chicken that can't feather itself ought to freeze to death."

Unlike many Negro preachers of his day, the elder Borders did not shout his audience into an emotional frenzy and then dismiss them. The son had heard such preaching during his college days in Atlanta, before moving to Chicago and Northwestern University, where such pulpit practice was unthinkable.

However, when the elder Borders had quickened his delivery, the brothers and sisters had responded louder and louder. No doubt remained that the preacher was about to make his sermon point. Anticipation mounted.

Out of memory, the son could again see his daddy standing in the pulpit before him. Sweat glistened over the flat planes of his daddy's brow. Those big hands, that had held blacksmith tools during his slave days, gripped the edge of the pulpit as though he was ready to tear it apart. The voice rang with sincerity.

"Friends, you and me, we say we believe in God. That's right, isn't it?"

The congregation responded with loud "Amens," for the preacher's tempo had heated up.

"Now brethren, if we believes in God, then we knows God is here today . . . right here . . . right now . . . in this church! Um, um, mmmmm. . . . That right, brethren?"

The congregation responded to the preacher's critical tone

and moaned in unison. One of the deacons called out, "Preach, brother! Preach!"

"Now friends, if we believes in God . . . and if we believes God is right here . . . in this church, right now . . . with us today . . . um, um, mmmmm . . . then we can talk to him in our prayers, right here, right now, today . . . can't we?"

"Yes, Lord!" sang the congregation.

"How do I know this? Know that Jesus is right here with us today? Why it's written right here!"

Triumphantly the preacher waved aloft his timeworn Bible for all to see. "Right here in Matthew twenty-eight, Jesus says that where two or three are gathered together in his name . . . there I will be also. It says that right here in my Bible. . . . Jesus says it in your Bible too. Don't he, brethren?"

While the preacher mopped the perspiration from his face with a white handkerchief, the congregation cried out, "Yes! Yes! Yes!"

"Then, brothers and sisters," and his daddy would lean forward to deliver the thrust of his sermon, the point he wanted to lie uneasy on their minds all week, "then brothers and sisters, if we believes God is here . . . in this church . . . now . . . today . . . um, um, mmmmm . . . if we really believes this, brothers and sisters, how come we don't act no different than we do? If we really believes, we'd act different, wouldn't we, huh?"

There would follow an awful wailing and crying, and several of the sisters would become a bit too happy and fall screaming in an emotional, hysterical, jerking heap on the floor.

This type of country preaching had led young Borders to the ministry. This was not the polished and structured form of preaching taught in his homiletics class at the seminary. Yet when he had been frightened by his failures, when he'd been a preacher who couldn't preach, he had not turned for help to the higher education of the seminary, but to the simple faith of his daddy and such contemporaries as Little William.

In his childhood days in rural Georgia there had been a saying, "A man must know where he's been before he can see where he's going."

Today Borders found this true, even though the course ahead was a bit blurred. As a handyman of the Lord he would serve as directed. He only awaited marching orders. He knew that all over America the Negro was restless, was marching, but he also knew that not all Negroes were marching to Zion. This disturbed him, and as a minister of the gospel he felt called upon to pray to God for guidance.

In his life many experiences had shown him there was a God who answered prayers. The first incident that he remembered had occurred when he was nine. He had wanted a bicycle, an impossible luxury in a family of eight children whose daddy earned but forty dollars a month. Undaunted, he prayed for the bicycle for several years. Meanwhile he delivered newspapers at four dollars a week, giving his mother half of his earnings. The other half bought his clothes and financed other personal expenses. Still he managed to set aside fifty cents most weeks, and occasionally even a dollar. It took two years, but eventually he bought a brand-new bicycle for $52.50. Every penny had been saved from his earnings.

He had been sure then, just as he was sure now, that God had answered his bicycle prayer.

From such boyhood experiences had come the realization that God helps those who honestly try to help themselves. The secret was to keep prayer and work in proper balance. When he prayed, he prayed as though everything depended upon God. When he worked, he worked as though everything depended on himself. When he faced problems and made plans for the future, he planned as though everything depended upon both God and his handyman. He took comfort in knowledge that the boss man's third part was ready to lend a helping hand.

In this same front pew of the Swift Creek Baptist Church another major decision had been resolved through prayer. He had promised himself to the Lord as a preacher like his daddy, but on graduation from high school he had gone to work to support his father's family. Instead of picking peaches and cotton, as his family had always done each summer and fall, he worked regularly as a substitute mail carrier at the post office in Macon. He earned an average of $150 a month, and from these wages paid off the mortgage on the family home and fed and clothed his father's family.

Those were not happy days for young Borders. His father's failing health permitted only token work and an occasional preaching assignment. Most of his brothers and sisters were content to let their younger brother support them. This attitude eliminated the possibility of his discussing his problem with family members, although they all would share the effects of his decision. Nor did he have the experience or background to know how to cope with this problem.

Therefore, in this same front pew he turned to the Lord for guidance. However, the answer was not immediately revealed. Each day as he prayed, the young man told God that more than anything else in the world, he wanted to be a preacher. Then one day, after the baby of the family graduated from high school, and all his brothers and sisters were of working age, he suddenly knew what to do.

He told his father that he had saved enough money to

finance two years of college. He confessed that he had no idea where to turn for the rest of his college money, but that did not matter. His mind was made up. He was going to honor his promise to God. He was going to be a preacher.

Without a word, his father slipped off his money belt and emptied its contents on the table. There was $39.41.

"Son, this is all I have. Take it. And I'll pray for you."

Soon afterward Borders left Swift Creek Baptist Church and enrolled in Morehouse College in Atlanta. He never went back again to live there in the bottom of the hollow in Swift Creek, but these humble origins were part of him and never far removed from his conscious thoughts.

Now, as a man nearing fifty years of age, a preacher himself, he was again sitting in that same front pew. From his mind he erased those memories of yesterday, for the problems of the present were real. There was no question about the goals of the civil rights movement. The question was one of method and of the preparedness of his people to receive the freedom which was rightfully theirs, but which had been for such a long time denied them.

Just a few weeks before, he and his wife had visited the subcontinent of India. They had marveled at the courage of Mahatma Gandhi, and were amazed at the depth of his love for his enemies. Through nonviolence this wisp of a man had broken the political and economic fetters of a society which for centuries had made outcasts of the untouchables of India—the Harijan. Borders and his wife had talked to many of the Harijan. They discovered in these outcasts the same incubus of self-hatred and despair so often encountered among their own people here in America. The obvious conclusion was that people who are scorned, abused, and ignored, react similarly despite differences in race and in geographic location.

From Mahatma Gandhi's writings he recalled the sharp warning: "One day the black races will rise up like the avenging Attila against their white oppressors, unless someone presents to them the weapons of satyagrahi" [nonviolent resistance].

The round-the-world trip had been the gift of a grateful congregation to their pastor and his wife. During the Borders' two decades at the Wheat Street Baptist Church the congregation had grown from four hundred to more than five thousand members. A debt-laden and unfinished church structure, with only the basement occupied, had developed into one of Atlanta's finest church buildings. The church had no debt encumbrances.

During these years Borders had fought for jobs and homes and political and educational opportunity for his people. Given a chance, the black man could build and produce. He had seen this happen at Wheat Street. The dispirited had found hope, and with each collective accomplishment there had been added in each individual heart a stronger defense of pride and assurance. In his sermons he had preached: "Stand on your feet. You are made in the image of God, just a little lower than the angels. God loves you. God loves me. He said, 'There's room enough in heaven for all of us.' I believe him. Don't you?"

Through these years of struggle there had emerged within him an awareness of the sharp economic issue involved in civil rights. The issue was not just a question of black and white. It was also very much a question of black and white and green. Despite surface stories, the taproot of most race flare-ups was simply a question of money. Who would get the jobs? The best pay? White man? Black man?

Throughout his ministry Borders had been in the center

of the civil rights movement in Atlanta. In 1946, when four Negroes were lynched in nearby Monroe, Georgia, he went to that frightened and violent little village and arranged for the burial of the lynch victims with money he had raised. With nightly meetings in his church, he had also raised money and posted a $5,000 reward for information leading to the conviction of those responsible for this crime.

On his radio program he had lashed out at laws which stood for equal rights on the lawbooks, but not when they were enforced. He cited reports on police blotters, "Just another Nigger killin. No leads. Case closed."

"We have taxation," he had cried, "but we do not have equal rights and protection under the law."

He had led voter registration in Atlanta. Before the start of World War II, he had called on the mayor of Atlanta and advised him that there were five thousand registered Negro voters in the city. As the spokesman for a Negro citizens committee, he told the mayor they wanted a Negro policeman. The mayor replied, "You'll get a Negro policeman about as soon as you get a Negro deacon at the First Baptist Church" [a large all-white congregation]. Several months later he had again called on the same mayor, but this time with lists of an additional fifteen thousand registered Negro voters. The same mayor had said, "Reverend Borders, how many Negro policemen do you people want?"

Over his radio program he continually campaigned for social and political reforms: recreational areas for the entire city, not just in the Negro districts; equal salaries for Negro teachers; hospital care for the poor of both races. For this he had been called a Communist. Yet during the war he spoke out against racial extremists who claimed this was a white man's war. He had agreed with these extremists that the

Negro had grievances, but he advised his people to help America win the war and then win for themselves their American freedom. For this some Negroes called him an Uncle Tom.

In this volatile civil rights area, where sociological and political change was inevitable, he knew the stinging backlash from prejudices of both races. In this arena he knew that a man laid his career and his reputation on the line. Yet he had felt compelled to go on.

In his church and over the radio he spoke to his people of his beliefs: "We can't blame the white folks for all of our faults and all of our failures. We must admit we have our shortcomings too. But the white man must remember that although he has the bigger house, we all watch the same TV commercials. The desirability of the advertiser's product knows no race barrier. Those Negroes who want education and job training so they can earn a share of the fruits of a free democracy must be given that opportunity. Those white men who still hold to the old slave-servant relationship for the Negro must be proved wrong. Friends, we will prove such white men wrong; and what's more, we'll pray for them too. Give the Negro people the opportunity to earn for themselves the better life. Then it is up to the Negro people, up to you and me, to prove ourselves worthy."

Yes, the sting of a backlash could ruin a man's reputation and damage his career. However, Atlanta was his adopted city, Georgia his home state, these his people, this his country, and both races were the children of God. Today some of his people were muttering, "We'll take it!" or "It's ours!" or "We've a right!" These were subtle protests now, but not for long. He knew his people. "When you've lived all your life in a slum, you know even the names of the family dogs.

If every time you meet one of these dogs you kick at him, sooner or later he's going to slip up behind you and even the score." He had now to determine his own specific goals before these muttered protests became hardened attitudes, set in the mortar of public opinion.

He prayed.

2

All Uphill

At Morehouse College, William Holmes Borders was not an outstanding student. He worked long hours off campus, often was hungry, always tired, and he was constantly aware that his expenses were more than his earnings. The dreaded day when his money ran out occurred during the fall term of his third year. Unable to pay his college fees, he received notice to report at the office of the president, Dr. John Hope.

Dr. Hope was polite but firm. He closed the brief meeting with the words, "Son, I am sorry, but you will have to leave Morehouse."

However, young Borders continued to attend classes. Three weeks later he met Dr. Hope on the campus.

The president was furious. "Borders!" he roared. "I told you to leave."

"But Dr. Hope, I didn't have any money to go anywhere," was the reply.

Speechless with indignation, Dr. Hope turned on his heel. Borders continued attending classes.

This determination to graduate won him the friendship of Dr. Samuel Archer, dean of men. Archer made no promises, but he saw to it that the young man's class grades were posted and also that he was not denied access to the college library. Whenever they met, Archer always stated, "I can only officially advise you to go home." When Archer sent for him, there was always a practical reason. "Borders, I understand there's a few hours' work available at the freight terminal. Here's the name of the man to see."

Even with such help, those last two years at Morehouse College were increasingly difficult for Borders. He was down to two shirts. Fortunately, his roommate worked at the college laundry. Each week his roommate brought back four shirts, having borrowed two shirts from some other boy's laundry. The next week the two missing shirts would be returned and two more shirts would be borrowed from another boy's laundry.

Despite such struggles, his marks improved. Archer became more and more inquisitive about Borders' intentions after his college education. Before long he told Archer about his boyhood promise to God to be a preacher like his daddy.

After his final college grades were posted, Borders had better than average passing marks and a very sizable indebtedness to the college. On the morning that his class graduated, Archer took this determined but unauthorized student to the home of the president. That official was busy shaving and dressing, preparatory to giving his commencement address to the graduating class. Archer opened the touchy subject of Borders by admitting the case was unusual and suggesting that it be discussed with the young man himself. This was in the spring of 1929 and American colleges had had little experience with student loans and student aid.

Dr. Hope continued dressing and said hardly a word during

the twenty minutes or so that Archer talked. Finally, when his tie was tied and a red carnation was tucked in his coat lapel, the president turned to the insistent young man whom he had dismissed two years before.

"Borders, if I let you graduate, do you promise to pay back to Morehouse College all the money you owe?"

"Dr. Hope," Borders said, "if I've been in Morehouse College for four years and I don't want to pay my debts, there's something wrong with this college."

The president was only partially angry. "Borders, you talk like a fool," he said, but within the hour he handed the young man his diploma.

After the graduation exercises, Archer had a number of papers for his special graduate to sign. Among them was an application for a scholarship to Garrett Theological Seminary, Northwestern University, at Evanston, Illinois. Before the end of the summer, he was awarded the scholarship.

That fall Borders arrived in Chicago. He described the event as neither auspicious nor promising. "I had but six dollars, I was a Baptist in a Methodist school, and to make matters worse, a Negro in a white school."

However, during those first two weeks of class, one of his professors, Dr. Harris Franklin Rall, Professor of Systematic Theology, called him "Mister." Borders was twenty-four years old and no one had ever before called him "Mister." He doubted that any member of his family, including his daddy, had ever been called "Mister." "Something dead inside me came alive," is how he later described the experience. "Here was proof, from a learned white man whom I respected, that I was more than an animal. This white man saw me as a child of God, created in his image, and he knew that God loved me. I wanted to cry."

After class, frightened by his own awkward shyness and

insufficiency with words, he nevertheless sought to thank this white man. Dr. Rall promptly invited this new Negro student to stop at his house that afternoon for tea and an informal discussion with other students.

There were to be many such teas, for there quickly developed one of those student-professor relationships out of which creative learning grows. At that first meeting, however, Borders contributed little more than his presence. He listened in amazement as this learned man discussed with equal familiarity philosophy, literature, history, psychology, theology, and composition. He was later to learn that Rall was a meticulous grammarian who insisted that every theme must be soundly structured if it was worthy of a grade in any subject.

Another surprise occurred when Mrs. Rall asked her husband to make the lemonade. This learned man promptly sliced and squeezed lemons, adding measured amounts of sugar and water. He appeared to delight in stirring the lemonade. Borders, however, resented the time Dr. Rall took from the group's discussion. Yet the experience taught Borders a lesson which Dr. Rall himself made quite clear later. "Some of us have few practical talents," he explained. "I'm told I make good lemonade. So I nourish one of my few talents of the sort and am quite proud of the results."

This was a period when the theological pendulum in America was swinging toward liberalism and a concept called "the social gospel." Dr. Rall of Garrett Theological Seminary was one of the social gospel's leading spokesmen.

Advocates of the social gospel had an abiding preoccupation with human betterment. They were constantly probing man's environment in search of ways to improve man's lot. This led them to see man's goodness and to make excuses for his sins. This apology for sin brought a de-emphasis of such personal and traditionally evangelistic experiences as conversion and sanctification.

The social gospel follower also had a tendency to lean heavily upon the biblical critic. Biblical criticism sought to understand the Bible by applying to its every verse "scientific methods of analysis." The method was quite similar to that used by the linguistic scholar to determine the authenticity of a poem by a study of style, vocabulary, references, apparent date of authorship, and similarities to other recognized works. Of course such an approach viewed the Bible as purely a human book, shorn of the orthodox view that the Scriptures were divinely inspired.

For the young Negro lad, whose background was one of simple faith in the Bible as the authoritative word of God, these new ideas caused some uneasy moments. Hadn't his daddy preached, "I know it's true. It's written in my Bible." Yet the son now heard fellow students question whether the Gospel account of the raising of Jairus' daughter might not be wishful thinking of the early church, rather than an actual event.

Patiently Dr. Rall explained to his startled protégé that seminary students, when pushing a new point of view to its limit, often reached extreme and unorthodox conclusions. As he talked, Rall worked cautiously to unlock the fixed viewpoint of young Borders. He pointed out that the biblical stories which young Borders revered as historical fact, as gospel truth, were also sociological truths just as meaningful today as when originally written.

These daily encounters with social gospel theology caused Borders to sharpen his own beliefs and to find definitive expressions of his own faith. From notes about the social gospel made in class, he wrote an essay expressing his point of view on one of the more controversial passages of scripture: "For unto us a child is born, unto us a son is given: and the government shall be upon his shoulder: and his name shall be called Wonderful, Counselor, The mighty God, The everlasting Father, The Prince of Peace" (Isa. 9:6).

Borders wrote:

> Few, if any, higher critics will agree that this verse refers to Jesus. Since they hold that everything in religion which cannot survive scrutiny should be discarded, that religion might enjoy intellectual respectability, they easily conclude that it is unreasonable for a prophet to predict the coming of Jesus eight hundred years prior to his arrival.
>
> However sure a higher critic is that religion and reason are practically synonymous, one finds in true religion, faith, mystery, and emotion—all of which defy and go beyond reason. Not only do they transcend reason, they discover knowledge, which is a form of reason apart from scientific method.... Nobody in any realm has a monopoly on truth, therefore, the higher critic may not be taken too seriously, nor should the foolishness of preaching be taken too lightly.
>
> If not according to the standards of higher criticism, then according to poetic beauty, Isaiah declares unto us a child is born, unto us a son is given. This is a message of hope in a dark world of despair. Pride and hypocrisy from within, fear and intimidation from without, have caused Israel's knees to knock and her teeth to chatter. God told Isaiah to put the word out that a child would be born, strange, wonderful, mysterious, who would be a star of hope.

In homiletics class the young man from the South found the struggle continued. Most of the sermons of his fellow students were not like anything he had ever heard before. In turn, his sermons, undoubtedly, sounded a new note to both students and professors.

One set of sermon notes prepared for homiletics class reads as follows:

Religion is real by experience. The blind man met Jesus and came forth seeing. Some tried to get the blind man's case history. Let us check with his parents. Some psychologist tried to pronounce it some form of dementia. He believed the boy was a mental patient.

The doubters said, I doubt that it happened. The discreditors said, it happened, but magic can't last. The diehards said Moses didn't do it, so Jesus couldn't do it. The hard-to-understands said it is a mystery to us; we ought to find this blind man and make him out a lie.

They found the blind man, and he said: "Whereas I was blind, now I see."

If you can quote your Einstein in mathematics, if you can quote your Kant in philosophy, if you can quote your Dewey in education, if you can quote your Rockefeller in high finance, why can't I quote my Abraham on faith? My Moses on leadership? My Job on patience? My Paul on grace? And my Jesus on love?

Despite this intellectual struggle, life at the seminary was good. Borders immersed himself in the great literature of the ages, wherein man revealed the depth and clarity of his thinking. The more he probed those new avenues of learning, the sharper became his desire to help his people. If he was now actually escaping from the bondage of the past, what must his people, those in Georgia, what must they do to escape their present-day bondage of ignorance and poverty?

As the other students became better acquainted with this southern Negro traditionalist, Borders was often the focal point of class debates, especially in Dr. Rall's systematic theology class. To maintain his side of the arguments required more and more Bible study. One evening as he walked on the campus with Dr. Rall, and they discussed the overriding impressions the Bible left on their minds, he suddenly found himself giving a ringing affirmation to Cain's angry question, "Am I my brother's keeper?" He saw that from Genesis to Revelation the Bible gave a positive answer to this question. As God's handyman he must preach the gospel and also labor to be his brother's keeper. Both prospects were to his liking. There were other tests also.

To pay for his meals, he cleaned a fraternity house on the campus of Northwestern University. During the summer months only a few men remained at the fraternity house. One morning he entered a room to clean it and discovered three dollars in change lying on the windowsill.

"I put that money in my pocket, and immediately telephoned the man who lived in that room. I called him at his place of work. I did not want to wait for him to come back to the fraternity house. I wanted him to know that I had the money, the exact amount, which I would keep for him. He thanked me, and when he returned that afternoon, he told me to keep the money. He said he was glad to be able to trust his room to me."

Young Borders was certain that this man had been testing his honesty. From the start he was confident that he was handling the situation correctly, and this assurance he attributed to his father's training.

"There was always a great need for money around my father's house, but there was never enough money to meet the needs. My father taught me, however, that the main thing about money was honesty. I believed this when he taught me. I knew my father was right when this incident occurred at the university. Now, I know that he was absolutely correct."

While attending Morehouse College, Borders had met Julia Pate, who was studying at neighboring Spelman College. Then when he was in Evanston studying theology, the young woman was at the University of Chicago on a Julius Rosenwald scholarship, earning her master of arts degree in English literature and sociology. They saw each other so frequently in the Windy City that when she returned to Atlanta to teach at Spelman College, he felt lost and alone.

During the Christmas vacation of 1931, he rushed to Atlanta and they were married, although the bride could not return to Evanston until June when she had finished the terms of her teaching contract. However, theirs had been a courtship of six years, and the romance of that courtship and early marriage never completely died.

Borders received his bachelor of divinity degree from Garrett Theological Seminary in 1932, and a year later earned his master of arts degree. He had also accepted the pastorate of the Second Baptist Church, in Evanston, which offered a weekly salary of twenty-five dollars, a parsonage, and an opportunity to continue his studies for his doctorate.

His first step was to send for his father.

"I had spent my early years with him at his church and in our home. I had only been away from him during my school days at Morehouse College and at the seminary. Now that he had retired, I felt that he needed me. I thought it was my privilege to care for him, while in reality he continued my training."

During those early days in the pastorate at Evanston, the elder Borders exerted a great deal of influence upon the young preacher. This was never done in public, it was never done openly, or in the sense of intruding with direct advice. However, it was done in such a manner that the desired truths to be gained from an experience became evident.

"I remember," recalls Borders, "that once he asked the name of my choir director. I told him the man's name, and immediately he said this man would give me trouble. I said, 'Oh, no, Papa. That will never happen.' About two years later there was conflict, and, of course, the director left. Noting the choir director's absence for several Sundays, my father asked me about it. I said there had been a misunderstanding and I had all but forced his resignation.

"My father nodded. 'I told you that man would give you trouble.'

" 'How were you sure of this?' I asked.

" 'I looked at him,' the old man replied, 'I watched that man's actions with you and with other people. He did not treat everyone alike. I thought about this, and I prayed about that man, and it was revealed to me that he would cause you trouble.'

"Now I am not saying that the preacher in this case, meaning me, was absolutely right or the choir director absolutely wrong. I am saying that my father had remarkable insight, was very, very prayerful. He did not believe you could deal with people, even in your own church, unless you studied them, thought about them, and prayed over them.

"It is a legacy which every father would do well to pass on to his son."

By the standards of his youth, Borders had already achieved more than he had dreamed possible. He had a church, a good income, a home, a lovely wife, and there was soon to be a family of his own. He had won achievements and honors in an intellectual world whose very existence he had not previously known. However, everything was not perfect. His studies went well, his marriage was a blessing, but all was not well at the church.

When he had taken over the Second Baptist Church there had been a heavy indebtedness. In three years he cut that indebtedness in half and reestablished the church's credit. He was active in the local Interracial Council and on the board of directors of the Evanston Consumers Cooperative. Yet the church did not grow, and in the congregation he sensed a rising resentment directed toward the preacher. As he sought the reason for this, he was quite aware that he had harassed the church members about the debt, but also he had to admit that his sermons were putting his congregation to sleep.

"The sophistication of seminary years and training had moved me away, or so I thought, from my humble, early experiences," he now recalls. "I was engrossed in my new world of intellectualism. I had started thinking as an intellectual. I had turned from the simple, sincere biblical message of hope so familiar to my people. I was preaching from where I thought I was, and not from the level of interest and knowledge of my people. I wanted to teach them all the cultural discoveries I had made and they wanted to hear me explain the promises of the Scriptures.

"I had taken things into my own hands, and I had made myself into a preacher who couldn't preach. I was frightened. I had responsibilities, a wife and two precious children, and a father past eighty years of age.

"My ability to hold my own, and to be accepted, in the intellectual circle of this great school; the experience of being treated equally by my white associates, had built within me a sense of false pride. I was all puffed up with my own importance. But suddenly I was frightened, afraid that I was failing. I felt naked and ashamed before my God.

"Remember how God called to Adam in the Garden of Eden, 'Where art thou?' I felt God calling me then. Like Adam, I was ashamed to answer. Finally, after my family had all gone to sleep, I got to my knees and confessed my errors and prayed for his forgiveness.

"After that first traumatic prayer experience, I felt better.

I had the same problem, but I knew that I would not face my problem alone: God's third part, our overseer, would be with me."

In his now-frantic haste to return to the ways of his people, Borders worked hard at writing poetry. He tried to depict the biblical truths learned at the seminary in the words of Little William, and all the other uneducated Negro preachers who had taught his generation. He knew that he had to return to the colloquial expressions of men such as his daddy, but he found little help at the seminary. When he showed his literary efforts to his friend Dr. Rall, the latter quickly pointed out, "I have no way to evaluate them. It is out of my kind of experience."

Conditions at the church had now reached a point where he feared the Board of Deacons would ask him to leave. Then in early July, 1937, he received a letter from Morehouse College inviting him to be an instructor on the faculty. The idea that he would be leaving the intellectual environment of Northwestern University and the seminary was disconcerting, but he had no will to flaunt this opportunity to escape a failing situation.

He discussed the letter with Dr. Rall.

"It's a great honor for your own college to ask you to return," his instructor pointed out. "You have learned much here. However, that knowledge will be more real to you once you have had time to organize it, present it, and teach it. There will be time enough to complete work on your doctorate degree later, if you should decide to pursue that course." So Borders resigned the pastorate of the Second Baptist Church on September 4, 1937, and took his family back to Atlanta.

As an instructor at Morehouse College he taught freshman classes a general course in the Bible and a course in

Christian ethics; and in the School of Religion he taught a course in the philosophy of religion. His salary was $160 a month, and his wife resumed her teaching position at Spelman College at a like salary.

There was much to do. They prepared their teaching courses, got settled in their new Atlanta home, and sought to re-establish roots in the Southland. Underneath this activity there was a growing sense of contentment. The decision to leave Evanston had been right. They could go back later, but for the present this was their life.

Such complacency, however, was short lived. At an early faculty meeting, the question of teacher retirement was discussed. The college offered a new proposal. Borders asked if the plan included the college's janitors and caretakers. When advised it did not, he protested. "We have more knowledge and know-how than they do. Therefore our ability to support ourselves in later years is greater than theirs. They should be covered."

Much later the matter was resolved by the inclusion of all custodial help in the pension plan. However, the incident disturbed him for it had revealed a failure. He had promised God to be both a preacher of the gospel and his brother's keeper. He was now living up to but half of his promise.

Just to the east of Atlanta's business district spread an extensive Negro slum. In this slum, at the southwest corner of Auburn Avenue and Fort Street, there was a discouraging and pathetic church situation. The historic and once prosperous Wheat Street Baptist Church had started the most ambitious building program of any Negro church in Atlanta. Construction had been well under way when the great depression and subsequent bank failures wiped out every dime of the church's building fund and even the operating funds. The blow had been too much for the Reverend Peter James

Bryant, who died in 1929. He was followed in the pulpit by the Reverend J. Raymond Henderson, who conducted services in the cavernous basement of the unfinished church structure.

Henderson, a man of good college background and many abilities, struggled with the situation for seven years. He managed to pay off $29,000 of the indebtedness, and then resigned.

The Board of Deacons was not looking only for a new pastor but also for someone to preach on Sunday. The new instructor at Morehouse College, who had had all that training up North, was invited to preach.

The original Wheat Street Baptist Church was well known to Borders' father. It had been built of materials salvaged from the fiery aftermath of the Battle of Atlanta. It had been a simple structure of barren pine-board walls and roughhewn benches for pews. The building had stood alone in a wheat field beyond what was then the end of Auburn Avenue. Although officially named the Mount Pleasant Baptist Church, the congregation of freed slaves, most of whom could not read, were soon calling this meetinghouse "the Wheat Street Church." This colloquial name, later officially adopted by the church, had survived until the present. Now the church's once proud membership had dwindled to less than four hundred members. People openly scoffed at the grand plans for a large modern sanctuary, now represented only by the enormous basement room beneath its tarpaper roof.

Here Borders preached for two Sundays. He preached as he had preached in Evanston and the results were quite similar. One member of the church's official board tartly advised him that he needn't bother to come back, and others were equally unenthusiastic. He had intended to show these home folks what all that northern training had done for him, and instead he had shown them a Negro preacher who couldn't preach.

Resentment and frustration, like twin shadows, plagued his thoughts.

Shortly, however, an incident occurred which caused him to turn to the Lord in prayer, for it indeed put his back up against the wall. A white preacher in Atlanta, a man of rich college and seminary background, frequently spoke of his love of the arts and his desire to share this interest and knowledge with younger pastors. Borders called on this minister in the hope that they might read and discuss together some of the newer writings in their field. In the back of his mind there was still the happy memory of the seminary, the joy of pure learning. Still quite alive was the hope of returning to that intellectual fellowship, there to continue work on his doctorate.

His anticipation of renewed intellectual fellowship was short lived. The white minister subjected him to a form of denominational colonialism. He advised Borders pointedly that no white church in Atlanta would condone or understand such racial intermingling on the part of its pastor.

This rebuff angered Borders. It also sent him home intent on asking the Lord for a way out of this situation. Having once known the joys of civil freedom, he did not now relish the thought of slipping back into the traditional mold of southern servitude. Yet before getting down on his knees, he hesitated. He wanted to answer this problem in his own way, in anger. He shuffled through his papers for ideas, but all he found were some notes made in Evanston while writing poetry in the familiar old words used by Little William.

After his prayer, he telephoned the board member of the Wheat Street Church who had told him that he need not bother to come back. He knew, because of the church's unhappy situation, that the Board of Deacons was having a difficult time getting men to fill the pulpit each Sunday, much less to heed a call to the church itself. He did not apologize or explain, but simply told his reluctant listener that he would like to preach again at Wheat Street Baptist Church.

He had made up his mind that he wanted this pulpit. His previous attitude had been that if Henderson couldn't make the situation work, what could *he* do? He felt differently now. He had a challenge to meet, a personal challenge. He prayed that he would be made worthy to meet it. Between work on the sermon that he was certain he would be asked to preach, he worked on the poem inspired by Little William.

For his sermon topic, he chose "True Religion," and the text was Psalm 1:1-2: "Blessed is the man that walketh not in the counsel of the ungodly, nor standeth in the way of sinners, nor sitteth in the seat of the scornful. But his delight is in the law of the Lord; and in his law doth he meditate day and night."

For his introduction he defined several types of religion, among them, tribal religion, state religion, Sunday religion, and real religion.

Being mindful to stay within the areas of the congregation's experiences, he sought to illustrate each point by example.

"We all know," he said, "that some white people who profess Christianity practice tribal religion, a brotherhood of whites only."

There was a stirring in the congregation.

He illustrated this point by the story of a Negro who was hungry. He had been denied an education, political and economic opportunity, and was forced to beg for food. He rang the front doorbell of a southern mansion and the owner of the house answered. "I'm hungry," the Negro said. "Go around to the back door," he was told.

Food was prepared, and the owner of the house brought it to the Negro. "First we will bless the food," the white man said. "Now you repeat after me, 'Our Father . . .' "

The Negro said, "Your Father . . ."

"Why do you insist upon saying 'Your Father,' when I keep telling you to say 'Our Father'?" the white man asked.

The Negro beggar replied, "Well, boss, if I say 'Our Father,' that would make you and me brothers, and I'm 'fraid the Lord wouldn't like it, you makin' your brother come to the back porch to get a piece of bread."

The congregation was with him now and he hastened on.

"But we can't just blame the white folks. There are those of us who have Sunday religion just like we have Sunday clothes. For six days each week our Sunday clothes and our Sunday religion both hang in the closet.

"Some of us think a church is real estate, money, location, class, intellectual respectability, tall steeples, and heavy bells. I say that if we think that, we think like the Pharisees. The leading church in any town is the one that has the most religion, real religion. It believes in the brotherhood of all men, and it teaches the good life as righteous living for the pure of heart. Its worship service is holy and fiery. Its supreme power is God, its final and ultimate standard, Jesus, its objective the redemption of mankind.

"Friends, we don't want any substitute for real religion at Wheat Street Baptist Church. I remember in my daddy's country church a visiting preacher whom we called Little William. He didn't want any substitutes for the real thing. He prayed like this:

> 'Lord, help me to do right so that you can trust me with
> thy kind of power.

Help dying men to fall out with the ways of the world.
Let the sparks of religion fly from thy burning altar,
And catch our souls on hallowed fire.
Help me run this meeting like you want it.
Come, Lord, and walk up and down the aisles; don't send Mary, Luke, John, or Martha. I want you to come yourself, conquering King.' "

In Evanston he had forgotten the Altar Call, but not today.

"There is somebody here who believes the Old Testament says somebody is coming; there is somebody here today who believes the New Testament says somebody is here. There is somebody here today who believes the Bible in a peculiar way says there is a God. There is somebody here today who believes, but is not a member of a church. You ought to join God's church. Old man! Young girl! Christ is all! Come on and join God's church!"

The deacons stood up to receive those persons who responded to the Altar Call.

After service his father slipped an arm around his son's shoulder. "Son, today you became a preacher."

On November 17, 1937, Borders was called to the Wheat Street Baptist Church. He accepted.

3

The Tests

DURING THE FIRST MONTH that the Reverend William Holmes Borders was at the Wheat Street Baptist Church three separate events which were of unique and far-reaching consequence to him occurred. If he had approached any one of these events with anything less than an attitude of Christian charity, or had otherwise misjudged the situation, serious harm to his career might have resulted. One could have cost him his life.

However, at the moment his concern was for a failing church, whose dwindling membership was still drifting from the fold. The loyal core of the congregation, he discovered, was for the most part discouraged, apathetic, and less interested in achievements on earth than in promised rewards in heaven.

One day, after a discouraging study of the membership lists of the church, he closed the door to his office study and walked down Auburn Avenue. After a few blocks he was in the heart of the Negro business district. The sight of a barbershop reminded him of the promise made to his wife that morning to get a haircut. He entered the nearest barbershop and introduced himself to the barber as the new pastor at the Wheat Street Baptist Church, just down the street.

The barber nodded, motioned him to a chair, but said nothing at first.

Without warning, the barber suddenly asked, "Reverend Borders, do you think there really is a hell?"

Not waiting for a reply, the barber proceeded to answer his own question. "There can't be no hell. If there was a hell, you preachers would be doing things different, wouldn't you?"

Since he had never before met the barber and was not quite certain if the man's question stemmed from a personal need or religious bias, he sought momentarily to delay a direct reply.

"On the other hand," he told the barber, "whether you or I believe in a hell or not, all men are ready to accept God's help, aren't we?"

The barber paid him no heed, as he continued asking and answering his own questions.

"If you preachers really believed in a hell, you'd be down the street—in the bars and poolrooms, telling those no-goods what hell is really like. You'd tell them they ain't seen nothin' yet."

Escaping from the barbershop, Borders walked down Auburn Avenue. The slow climb out of the depression years had taken a turn for the worse. The economists called the period a recession, but the hurt in individual lives was no less severe. There were still WPA projects and CCC camps, there were food stamps and surplus-food bundles, and there were still far too few jobs. Men, homeless men, without resources or hope, drifted the streets. They hung around bars and pool halls, their rags and filth a uniform of failures and misfortunes. Fear and hurt were experiences too common to warrant notice. Only as one looked deep into the stormy pools of their eyes could you discern their abiding resentment at a life that offered them only more misery.

Borders hastened back to the church. The barber had been right about one thing. Those men needed a preacher. They wouldn't listen to a preacher tell them about the wages of sin being eternal damnation and hell, and in truth, what more could a preacher tell them? What these men needed was a preacher who would tell them that God loved them and forgave them and wanted them back in the fold.

In a work cabinet at the church he found the materials he sought. With paint and cardboard he made posters. Within an hour he was back on Auburn Avenue, his posters still wet with paint. This time he entered the bars and pool halls, sought out the managers and requested permission to nail up one of his signs. He was not turned down once.

Most of the signs were alike. "God loves you! There's a new preacher at Wheat Street. Come Sunday!"

After tacking up a poster, he would turn to face the incredulous or hostile stares of the homeless. He treated everyone alike.

"You forgot that God loves you, didn't you?" he asked. "God loves you and he'll never let you down if you trust him. And God will never let you escape him. Why? Because he's invested something in you."

Then he quickly told the story of Jonah, concluding: "When given a second chance, Jonah gave God a full return on his investment. Maybe it's time you turned to God for your second chance. See you at Wheat Street Church on Sunday."

Borders missed dinner that evening. Several hours later, to an upset wife, who was partially angry and partially proud, he said, "Jesus didn't come to save the righteous but those who sinned. I've tried. I'll keep on trying. I couldn't live with myself if I didn't try."

Next day he painted more signs and distributed them throughout the Auburn Avenue area. Men no longer looked surprised when they saw the preacher putting up his posters. They watched him closely. They wondered what this preacher's angle was, and what he wanted with them.

One old man said, "Preacher, you done made me feel better already. But we ain't got no Sunday clothes."

"Come as you are," he replied.

For the rest of the afternoon he went up and down Auburn Avenue, painting on his signs, "Come dressed as you are."

That evening he attended his first business session of the official board of the Wheat Street Baptist Church. He felt good inside. He was totally unprepared for the storm of protest he encountered.

Mrs. Gertrude Warren, a wealthy widow and one of the church's most generous benefactors, started the attack.

"I understand, Preacher, that someone has invited those people down on Auburn Avenue to attend this church on Sunday."

"Yes, I invited them," he said. "We've plenty of room. Those men need us. They need God's love. I hope some of them come."

"I don't!" Mrs. Warren thundered. "This church, the Wheat Street Baptist Church, is for the members of this church. The membership are respectable citizens. We don't beg for handouts and we don't reek of liquor. I don't expect to worship with the filth and riffraff from off the street corner."

Borders cut her short, his voice as sharp as hers.

"Sister, I'm sorry you said that. Let me correct a big mistake you made. Wheat Street Baptist Church is not the property of its members. We are but tenants. This is God's church. You hear me? It's God's church, not ours. And these unfortunate men are children of God. They're our own people too. I don't care if they don't have a clean shirt or tie. If they want to find God, they're welcome as long as I'm pastor of Wheat Street Baptist Church. Furthermore, Sister, I'd put those signs up in hell itself if I had a way back."

Picking up his hat and coat he walked out.

For the next several days he did not know if he was pastor of Wheat Street Baptist Church or not. He heard from no one in the church, but the news of the pastor's stand had reached Auburn Avenue. When he walked down that thoroughfare, men would touch their fingers to their caps, and a few mumbled an almost inaudible "Mornin', Preacher."

On Sunday morning Borders made his way through a mute congregation to his pulpit to deliver his first sermon as pastor of the Wheat Street Baptist Church. With a great deal of satisfaction he noted that in the back of the basement auditorium were seated a handful of Auburn Avenue homeless. Some had heeded his signs.

He divided the day's message into two parts. For those listeners in the back of the room he said: "Our question is, can we really place our trust in God? Can we believe in the power of prayer? Well, why not? We trust in everything else, the tipster, the numbers peddler, the sweepstakes ticket. And when our backs are right up against the wall and there's no possible way out, then we turn to God in prayer. Don't we?"

For those sitting stiffly, almost remotely, in the front pews, he said: "A church is indeed more than a social club. If we, as a people, as individuals, are to survive, we must strengthen our inner spiritual beliefs. We must believe in God. We must behave as though we believed in God. When we behave in his manner, we automatically broadcast God. When we do that, God will see to it that we have a real church."

After the service there were a few handshakes.

Years later Borders recalled this Sunday when asked to comment on news stories about certain of Atlanta's white churches which had refused to permit Negroes to worship in their congregations.

"Sometimes," he said, "we claim for ourselves that which rightly is the Lord's, even when we know better. Mrs. Warren knew it wasn't her church, but his church. She wanted to impose her will, not his will. Sometimes this happens even to fine, outstanding Christians like Mrs. Warren. I'm glad to say she came to me later, after she had prayed to the Lord for forgiveness. I'm proud to say she donated two of the large stained-glass windows for our new sanctuary.

"Now back to your question. If I've had such a problem in my own church, among my own people, I can't be too critical of those white brothers who falsely view his church as their church. Can I? I don't think so. But I can pray for all who make that mistake."

When Borders took over as pastor at the Wheat Street Baptist Church, he was quite aware that the level of financial giving had not been meeting current expenses. He talked about this to members of the church, to the Board of Deacons, and then he went to the Atlanta Police Department.

To pay off the church's indebtedness, the Reverend J. Raymond Henderson, during his seven-year tenure, had pushed the congregation hard. Since the church had had several times the amount of the indebtedness on deposit at the time of the bank failure, it was only natural that some members expressed resentment at "paying twice." Also, in the interval between Henderson's resignation and his own appointment, there had been a reported theft of funds at the Wheat Street Baptist Church. The Atlanta police had investigated. No one knew anything more, for the police had not reported back.

At the Atlanta Police Department Headquarters, Borders learned that the investigation had been closed with the notation "Inside job."

Armed with this information, the preacher again spoke to his deacons. He quickly became aware of an undercurrent of mistrust regarding all financial matters of the church. This feeling arose partially from a lack of anything approaching an adequate accounting practice, but had also been fanned to an uncomfortable degree by suspicions and accusations after the theft of church funds.

One of the intriguing and lovable facets of his seminary professor's personality was Dr. Rall's inability to stick to his subject of systematic theology. One of his pet deviations was the subject of a pastor's responsibility when handling church funds. "As pastor," he had told his students, "you are handling God's money. You are responsible for the collection and disbursement of every penny. You are accountable before God and your church to the last thin dime."

By his own investigation, Borders knew that a handful of people, including the church secretary, had access to what was called "privileged information." This was the information taken off the weekly offering envelopes, and showed exactly how much money each church member had contributed. The other portion of this privileged information was found in the church treasurer's bank deposit book and checkbook.

First, Borders called on the church treasurer and picked

up both the church's bank deposit book and checkbook. Then he asked the church secretary for her list of the church members' weekly offerings. Reluctantly she gave him a box containing this information.

After studying both documents, he told the church secretary what he wanted her to do. She refused. "It wouldn't be worth the paper it's written on," she said. "Besides, I don't think you can do that. I don't think the deacons would approve. Furthermore, I'm going home now." And she left the office.

Borders was not certain if the Board of Deacons would approve of what he was about to do or not. He was far from certain that the decision was his to make, but that detail did not halt him. That night he made a ledger sheet on which he listed all the church members alphabetically. After each name he wrote the exact amount of their church contribution that month. From the church treasurer's records, he listed the amount of funds deposited in the bank, and from the checkbook stubs made a list of all expenses. He listed the recipient of each check and the amount of that check.

At Morehouse College next day he had stencils cut and personally mimeographed enough copies of this monthly financial statement to give a copy to each member of the Wheat Street Baptist Church. On Sunday he had the ushers pass out copies to all persons present. From the pulpit he announced that additional copies were available in the church office.

He also called attention to the biblical verse quoted on the monthly financial statement: "Bring ye all the tithes into the storehouse, that there may be meat in mine house, and prove me now herewith, saith the Lord of Hosts, if I will not open you the windows of heaven, and pour you out a blessing, that there shall not be room enough to receive it" (Mal. 3:10).

The congregation's reaction was volatile. Most persons present thought they had contributed much more than the record showed. Surely the preacher didn't again intend to publish this privileged information. He advised one and all that he did, and that he expected them to tithe.

The following Sunday some new faces appeared in the congregation. After the preaching service these people asked for their copies of the monthly financial statement. Also, the church treasurer advised that the day's offering showed a welcome increase, almost the first such increase he could recall.

Twenty-five years later, when making application to borrow five million dollars, these monthly financial statements, showing church receipts and disbursements for a quarter of a century, were a vital factor in the approval of the loan.

After these two events the young pastor—he was thirty-two years of age—felt that he had met his baptism of fire. He was therefore totally unprepared for the next event.

In those days a trolley car ran down Auburn Avenue. One evening, as Borders climbed up the basement steps of his church to go home, he noticed a trolley car was halted in the middle of the next block. A mob of people surrounded it and blocked Auburn Avenue from curb to curb.

Instantly he was aware of something strange about this crowd. The people, several thousand in number, were tightly packed together. They were from the neighborhood. Where normally their voices would be loud and raucous, this evening everyone was strangely quiet. Not a word was being spoken.

The atmosphere was charged, tense, sullen, waiting. It foreboded violence. The keyed-up crowd appeared but to await a signal to release its pent-up hostility.

Running down the street, he reached the edge of the

crowd. Someone recognized him. "It's the new Wheat Street preacher. Let him through."

The crowd squirmed and held its breath and he slipped through a crack in the sullen wall of human bodies.

He emerged from the crowd at the front steps of the trolley car. Suddenly he realized why the mob had slipped the preacher through its ranks: he was wanted as a witness to testify to the justification of the mob killing all expected to take place momentarily.

The trouble, the cause of the mob's wrath, was a silent drama being enacted at the front of the car. A Negro soldier, wearing the uniform of the United States Army, had tried to leave the streetcar by the front door. The white motorman had challenged him and now held the soldier pinned against the side of the door, a pistol jammed into the soldier's stomach.

The hated segregation laws of the South had been challenged, but the pastor felt the need for a moment to collect his wits. He asked the obvious question.

"Who are you?" growled the angry motorman. However, the motorman's voice cracked and seesawed at an uneven pitch. Borders realized that the man was truly frightened. He had a right to be afraid. That crowd wasn't mad at the soldier.

Someone from the crowd shouted that this was the pastor from the church up Auburn Avenue.

Like a floodtide, the words flowed from the motorman. "This nigger broke the law. He tried to leave by the front door. He knows better. He's no good. He's just trying to break the law. I'm pledged to uphold the law. I will, too. I'll shoot him if he don't obey the law. And that mob can't stop me," he added in a flat, sullen tone.

"No, I guess they can't," Borders replied. "However, once

you shoot this boy, nothing on earth is going to save you from that mob. They're going to tear you apart, limb by limb."

Then he turned to the soldier. The boy's cap was on the floor. The preacher picked it up and handed it to him.

"Son, you don't want to get shot. Do you? Not for the likes of him. You're worth a lot more. Now why don't you just put on your cap. Gentle now. Then you walk through this car to the rear door and just get off."

The soldier was frightened, and he had due reason to be afraid. Also, he was angry. A century of servitude, of discrimination, had boiled over. Carefully, slowly, he measured the situation as he placed his cap on his head. There was hatred in his eyes as he glared at the motorman, and that hatred was returned. When the soldier looked at him, Borders shook his head. "You got a lot of living to do, son. You don't want to die." Gently he took the soldier by the shoulder and started him down the aisle of the trolley car toward the rear door.

When he got the soldier to the door, he shouted to the motorman, "Open this door quick."

He shoved the soldier out the door and shouted to the motorman, "Close both doors. Tight. Now stand on that bell of yours. Keep sounding it. Move this car down the street before this mob turns us over."

The motorman clanged his bell. Borders stood beside him and waved for the mob to disperse.

Slowly the crowd opened, drew back, and the trolley car inched down the tracks until there was open space ahead.

"Go as fast as you can," Borders ordered.

The motorman did as he was directed.

When they were beyond reach of the mob, Borders told the motorman, "You can stop here."

As the trolley came to a halt, Borders reached over and tripped the lever opening the front door. Without a backward glance, he stepped off the trolley by way of the forbidden front door, the same door forbidden to the Negro soldier, forbidden to all members of his race.

The story of how the new pastor at Wheat Street Baptist Church stopped a riot and saved a soldier's life spread through the Negro quarter of Atlanta. By this same word of mouth those people had heard how Borders had invaded the dives along Auburn Avenue and had invited the people there to come to church. They had also heard that he stood up against those of his church who protested this action. They knew that he had tackled the question of privileged information at the historic old church and had scored another victory.

These stories added to the community's natural curiosity to hear this young preacher who had gone to school up North. New people who had never before been to Wheat Street Baptist Church started attending Sunday services. The basement auditorium filled up.

Thus, within the first month of his tenure as pastor at the Wheat Street Baptist Church, three events were thrust upon Borders. The manner in which they were handled reversed a negative trend in church attendance, in financial giving, in the attitude of the congregation. Wheat Street Baptist Church was back in the business of serving the Lord.

4

Real Religion

THROUGH no conscious effort on his part, the Reverend William Holmes Borders had been positively projected into the full awareness of the community. Far from being unmindful of this good fortune, he deliberately sought to capitalize upon it. He set out to organize his church service as completely, thoroughly, and prayerfully as he knew how.

He was only mildly aware that this organization stemmed less from his seminary training than it did from the recollections of his daddy's church services and those sermons he had heard preached by the Little Williams of his boyhood. Later he said: "I could never go back to the gummy emotionalism of those preachers of my youth. I wanted a clear, intellectually solid, gospel message. But I had had enough pulpit failures to realize that I must reach my people through the familiar forms of worship which they revered and understood. Once I had caught the attention and thoughts of my congregation, then I could commence feeding them the grains of spiritual truth and maturity I so keenly felt my people needed."

The first step to capture the attention and minds of his people was a one-hundred-voice choir. In a church of but four hundred members, there obviously weren't that many good voices available—even among the Negro race. Therefore the pastor with his deacons called on everyone in the neighborhood who was known or thought to have a good singing voice.

"I wanted my people to be thrilled with our gospel hymns that speak to us in our traditional idiom. If the hymn had a long, slow meter, I wanted the congregation to sway to its beat; if it had a short, rapid beat, I wanted them to tap their feet in unison. I wanted our music to do something to the worshiper in the pew."

Today at Wheat Street Baptist Church there are four choirs, representing several hundred voices. One choir is the Gospel Choir, which still sings such traditional gospel music as:

> I don't possess a house or land,
> fine clothes or jewelry;
> Sorrows and cares in this old world,
> my lot seems to be;
> But I have a Christ, who paid the price
> way back on Calvary.

Next, this young pastor wanted a Sunday school and children in the church. There were plenty of children in the neighborhood, but not in Sunday school. The problem was a lack of teachers, even untrained teachers. Since it would take a while to train Sunday-school teachers, he momentarily shelved that idea. Instead, he called his children the Gospel Chanters, and personally taught them verses from the Psalms. On Sunday he would march his line of children to the front of the congregation; while the piano was played softly, the Gospel Chanters would recite that week's memory work.

As the children returned to their seats, the pastor would address himself to the congregation. "Aren't they wonderful! Simply wonderful! They're your kids and mine. 'Blessed are the pure in heart: for they shall see God.' "

Today, with the Sunday school numbering in the hundreds, the Gospel Chanters remain an integral part of almost every Sunday service.

However, Borders' greatest change was to be his approach to the sermon. "My problem was to spread the gospel's good news down to the pews. Religion must reach into the lives of the people if it is to have a meaning to them. The church must love man as Christ did. When man is struggling against self-extinction, life has absolutely no meaning until he can feel the reality of God's love. A man who has found hope will respond to God."

In many of the people then attending Wheat Street Baptist Church there was recognizable the same self-hatred that this pastor and his wife were later to see in the untouchables of India. As a race, American Negroes had been told so frequently, by so many authorities, that they were no good, that often they did not think much of themselves. When a man doesn't think much of himself, he is living in a peculiar modern type of hell. He certainly is in no frame of mind to welcome the pastor harping on his failures or the fact that he is on a course hell-bent for eternal damnation.

By this line of reasoning, Borders ruled out most of the negativism in his daddy's old fiery sermons. "Let the old folks define sin," he said. "I'm preaching that Jesus loves us. He said there's room enough in heaven for us all. I believe him, brother. I believe him. Don't you?"

Some of his fellow ministers wondered about this approach and asked if it was best for their people.

"A preacher must lead his people," contended Borders. "It has been thus since the days of Moses. Moses led the children of Israel through the wilderness that they might be ready to enter the promised land. The same is true today. A preacher must lead his people. He must prepare them for a better life tomorrow." Then, with a twinkle in his eye, he countered, "I come from the farm, and I just don't recall having seen a horse push a wagon; do you?"

The neighborhood's reaction to the "leading" of the new young preacher at Wheat Street Baptist Church was tremendous. People came out of curiosity to see and hear "this northern preacher," and stayed out of conviction. The preacher's reaction to his enthusiastic and responsive congregation was equally dramatic. He meant every syllable when he told them, over and over again: "You're the finest people in the world. I love you. You've done wonders for me."

The more he talked to his congregation this way, the greater the number who came back for more. He described those initial sermons as "our courting time," and says: "If you burn long enough, someone else will catch on fire. If you love long enough, someone else will return that love."

However, his principal adviser remained his father. During those early years at Wheat Street Baptist Church they enjoyed their richest fellowship. His father occupied a room at the parsonage, and had a small remnant of a library with him. He also voluntarily shared family responsibilities. Church and civic meetings kept the young pastor out nearly every evening. Later he discovered that his father nightly made the rounds, checking to see that everything was secure. Also, he met his son after each meeting and saw that he reported his return to his family.

"This was a very kind and a very wise procedure. It kept me alerted, conscious of a family responsibility in addition to my responsibility to God himself. This training proved very fruitful in disciplining my personal behavior and reactions to my pastoral duties.

"During this time, indeed for his remaining years, my wife cared for my father. She did it so beautifully that at first I did not realize what was happening. When I realized what she had done, it was such a beautiful thing that it tied me to her the tighter. This was my father, not hers. But they came to understand each other with an infinite love that superseded the unity between myself and my father. Hers was a beautiful, a remarkable, service of love.

"Now, also, my father was my main advertiser. He would stand at the gate before the church and ask passersby, 'Do you know what church this is? Do you know the pastor of this church? My son is the pastor of this church. I want you to come here Sunday.'

"Not only did my father work up my crowd on Sunday, he was in the congregation. He almost never sat in the pulpit. As I preached, he would be the main 'Amen' responder in his immediate section of the church, and I could hear his voice saying, 'He's preaching now. That's my son. That's right, son. That's right. Go on and preach.' "

His father's enthusiasm was matched by that of the congregation. The only trouble was the overenthusiasm of some members. Where self-hatred had for a long period of time bottled up emotions, there was a bubbling over and near hysteria upon their release. An ushers' corps was quickly organized and stylishly uniformed (to establish their authority). The ushers were stationed in the aisles. Their duties were those normally performed by church ushers, plus the special duty of quieting down or escorting outside those members who became carried away by their happy emotions.

Today the decorum in the Wheat Street Baptist Church is not unlike that in most churches in America, with two individual exceptions.

One is Sister Bronner, who sometimes feels the Altar Call should be better attended. When she feels this way, Sister Bronner runs up and down the aisles exhorting others, "Get saved! Climb on board!"

The pastor grins and says: "Friends, that's Sister Bronner. She's an eighty-six-year-old lady, and she has to walk into church with the aid of a stick. But when she gets a calling to witness for the Lord, she can dance up these aisles just as spry as the youngest member here. She just loves the Lord, friends. We're mighty glad to have her at Wheat Street."

The other interrupter is a mite of a woman. She is normally so frail and shy of appearance as to pass unnoticed. However, if the pastor's sermon strikes her right, she punctuates his key points with loud "Amens" or a resounding "Praise the Lord."

Once in a while she becomes carried away with her role of responder. When this happens, Borders interrupts his sermon to say: "The word of the Lord sometimes gives Sister Hunter so much courage, she just has to sing out her praise. But I do wish one of the ushers would ask Sister Hunter if it would be all right for the preacher to continue the sermon."

Soon the preacher realized that his formal seminary manner of delivery was standing him in good stead. Even when he relaxed his style and method of delivery, he retained a more formal posture and manner than the Little Williams of old. He had achieved dignity and poise in the pulpit without sacrificing the informal and personal quality of worship that had so long characterized the Negro pastor and his congregation.

About this time a white woman came to see Borders. She explained that she was doing work among the deaf and hard-of-hearing. Only recently she had finished teaching some teen-agers in a white church how to use the sign language. These teen-agers were now translating the church service to a group of deaf persons. There was no other way, she explained, that the deaf could worship with fellow believers, and enjoy and take part in a Christian service. From the city's welfare agencies she had gathered a list of Negro persons who were deaf. She was quite positive the list was incomplete, that within the Negro community of Atlanta there were many deaf persons unknown to the agencies and, more important, unknown to the church. She had heard about Borders, and the things he was doing, from her Negro maid. Would he permit her to teach the sign language to members of his church so that the Negro hard-of-hearing might enjoy the privilege of attending church service with fellow believers?

He readily agreed, and six teen-age girls volunteered. At the conclusion of the training period—and it had been long and hard work for the girls—the announcement was made that the Wheat Street Baptist Church would simultaneously interpret its services for the deaf. The following Sunday morning nearly fifty hard-of-hearing persons arrived for church service. They were seated, as they are today, in the front pews to the left of the pulpit.

The interpreter stands before the group, her arms and hands and fingers moving rapidly as she keeps pace with sermon, hymn, or prayer. Twenty minutes is the maximum time for each of these girls, who take turns through services that often last over two hours.

The pastor's own daughter, Juel Pate Borders, when she did not want to return to boarding school, told her daddy: "Let me stay home, and I'll learn the sign language for the special class. I'll teach it to others." She was not quite in her teens at the time. Today she is a practicing physician, a gynecologist-obstetrician, with a family of her own, and she still teaches the sign language to those who volunteer to work with this special class.

Another extra service of the church started at this same time. Miss Etta Fountain came to the pastor and said she would like to organize an Auxiliary of the Matrons to conduct worship services in the county jail.

"When we started this experiment—it was 1938 or 1939, I believe—I did not have too much faith in it," Borders confessed. "But I was wrong. These ladies have done a tremendous task of witnessing for the Lord. I am now their strongest supporter. Here is a great program of the church. Miss Etta Fountain deserves most of the credit."

Every month this auxiliary goes to the prison and conducts a religious service. After the prisoners have served their terms and are released, many of these people come to see Miss Fountain, her auxiliary, or the pastor. The auxiliary and the church often take responsibility for partial rehabilitation, and in some instances obtain jobs for these former prisoners. Some of today's church members have changed the direction of their lives and have come to Wheat Street Baptist Church through the efforts of this auxiliary.

On occasion, the auxiliary also provides railroad fare for certain former prison inmates to return to their own homes. One grateful mother advised the pastor that her son was only thirteen years old when he hopped a freight and left their little town in western Tennessee. The boy spent most of the next ten years in jails, and when he did get home, usually stayed drunk. This mother had her minister write that after the Auxiliary of the Matrons had sent her boy home believing in the Lord, he found a job and now attends church regularly.

"Our batting average may not be the highest, but we're proud of our hits," is the way Borders describes the auxiliary's work.

By 1940 there was either a potluck dinner or a dinner served by one of the auxiliaries following every Sunday service at Wheat Street Baptist Church, and the continued growth and outreach of the church did not escape the notice of those news media serving the Negro community. The activities of the church were well reported in the pages of the Atlanta *World*, the Negro newspaper. The pastor and the publisher-editor, C. A. Scott, became close friends. An invitation to speak regularly over a local radio station served to project Borders into the next phase of the church's growing impact on the community.

He had only twelve actual minutes of radio speaking time each Sunday evening, and this limited time necessitated a complete new approach. He would not be speaking just to members of his own church, and possibly not just to members of his own race. There was no time to prepare for a worshipful attitude through music, and the station did not want just another radio sermon. He had just twelve minutes in which to say something meaningful, purposeful—to this community, his community, to the whole of the city of Atlanta.

He recalled a walk at the seminary when he had defined to Dr. Rall a double function of the Negro pastor: to preach the gospel and to be his brother's keeper.

At the radio station he laid out the format for the program. The talk would be social in approach, Christian in attitude.

It would cover all aspects of life in Atlanta, but from the distinct viewpoint of the Negro. There was nothing quite like it on the air in Atlanta at the time. Officials at the radio station were doubtful, and warned that listener ratings would determine the program's future.

The radio program had its inaugural broadcast in the days when World War II had already started in Europe, but this country had not yet become involved. Northern factories were crying for labor. The Negro community, segregated and discriminated against in much of the South, wondered about its opportunities in the North. One of the first radio topics was "Should the Negro Leave the South?"

This, Borders pointed out, depended as much on the person as on the seemingly better conditions for the Negro in the North. Some Negroes would go North and succeed and others would fail. A majority, he predicted, would stay in the South and also fail, while a few would succeed in spite of segregation.

"The opposition of segregation will produce tougher character, taller Christians, better citizens, a greater race. With stronger faith and clearer minds we will succeed. I cast my vote with those who feel called upon to dig in, grapple with the problem, knowing that the future is mortgaged to God, democracy, and Christianity."

Those were strong words for a Negro preacher to put on the airways of Georgia in the beginning of 1941.

Another early radio talk dealt with the increasing crime rate in Atlanta. Borders listed the causes for the increase of crime as lack of recreational facilities, low wages, dilapidated housing, ignorance, lack of job training, lax law enforcement. He then proceeded to speak on each subject in the following weeks.

He was not bashful. He condemned the lack of recreational programs and facilities in all of Atlanta. Then he took his fellow Negro ministers to task. "We've too long condemned the unwholesome aspects of commercial amusement and recreation without proper thought and action to provide wholesome recreation to fill the needs of our people. We must guide the energies of our young people into creative channels. This is a responsibility of the church, but we must have help and support from the city of Atlanta."

There was a constant comparison of moneys appropriated for Negro and for white education in the state of Georgia. The Negro's inability to secure the vote was referred to as "taxation without representation."

The radio program quickly earned what one audience-listening service called the second highest rating of local or national radio programs in the Atlanta area.

The surprise was the number of white listeners. On some weeks their percentage approached a majority. One portion of the white audience was hostile, bitter. They called Borders a Communist, a northern agitator. He loved to reply that he was a native son of Bibb County, Georgia. However, a large part of the response from the white community indicated an appreciation of many, if not all, of his points of view. They asked that he continue the program because "it is opening communication between our races."

By now the United States was engaged in World War II. One night Borders spoke out strongly against those Negroes who advocated refusal to fight, on the ground that this was a white man's war. In his concluding remarks, he said, "After the war, let us, black man and white man, build in Atlanta a city for God. But don't wait till then to help my people. We need your help now."

The mail that came after this broadcast was unusually heavy. Many letters were written on the letterheads of large corporations and respected local business firms. In each instance the writer asked how he or his firm could help the Negro people as suggested in the broadcast.

From that moment on, Borders stressed jobs for his people, and another facet of the Wheat Street story unfolded.

"In every community there should be communication across racial lines, across all lines, as a matter of fact. I am not exactly sure how it happened," Borders says, "but I became something of a channel in directing people to jobs. This has been a great joy to me and a benefit to my people."

Other persons in Atlanta are more emphatic as to how this bridge between the races was established. Many white business executives subscribe to the Negro paper, the Atlanta *World*, in order to keep up with the Negro viewpoint on local issues. As pictures and stories of the Wheat Street Baptist Church and its new pastor had more and more frequent coverage, a favorable impression was formed. This was furthered and enlarged in a more personal manner by Borders' radio talks. Also, in many of Atlanta's better homes there are Negroes working as domestic help, and the opinions of these people on matters relating to their part of the city are often highly valued by their employers.

A Negro pastor is always besieged by his people who wish to use the pastor's name as reference when they seek employment. Often those turning to their pastor have just the strength of their bodies to offer, and sometimes not a great deal of that. Others with skills—cooks, waiters, gardeners, painters, carpenters, plumbers—need help to find work. Professional persons seeking teaching or church positions are in need of recommendations. For years the Negro pastor has been a job counselor to his people.

Soon more and more white business executives telephoned the pastor at the Wheat Street Baptist Church to inquire about needed labor. Borders realized he must set up an organization for this task. The result was an employment agency in the church. All persons out of work or having only temporary jobs were asked to fill in a reference card similar to those used in employment bureaus. Each applicant was personally interviewed by the pastor, who wrote out his comments, evaluating the employment potential of the person. As a result of this initial screening, many classes were started at the church on personal grooming, good manners, reliability, and honesty. In turn, if a job did not pay the going rate, Borders turned it down.

Some recent calls have been for as many as two hundred laborers, and the requests were met. Not all, but many, of these persons were first asked to report to the pastor, who gave a last bit of counseling.

One such laborer was Sam Brown, age fifty, listed as having an eighth-grade education, with a family of five children. This is how the pastor spoke to him:

"Now, Sam, here's the place of business and here's the name of the man you're to see. Sam, this man's work starts at eight each morning. You get there fifteen minutes early. You wash and shave and put on a clean shirt each day and get to work fifteen minutes early. Hang up your coat and hat and get to your place of work. This man has a lot of goods on his shelves, Sam. Some things you might like to have. But they don't belong to you, Sam, remember. They're his. He has to sell them if he's to make enough money to pay your salary. You want your salary? Then you leave his goods alone. It'd be stealing to take any of those goods, Sam. God doesn't like for us to steal. And Sam, Flora and your kids need that pay check. They need all of it, Sam. Every payday they need it. I've told your employer there's to be no salary advances. Also, I told him that if he ever sees you in a bar, during hours or after hours, he's to fire you, Sam. You know what I mean? If that happens, Sam, don't blame that white man, or me. The blame will be yours, because you couldn't leave the bottle alone. I've had to rustle up grub for your family before, Sam. It had better not happen this time."

The pastor watched as this middle-aged man clutched the employment slip and hastened from the room.

Borders shook his head. "Sometimes you just about reach the end of the rope," he said. "Sam's the quietest, most conscientious worker an employer could want. Then comes payday, and Sam has a buck in his pocket, and he just has to join the other boys for a quick drink. He usually stops when the money's gone."

The pastor suddenly turned to his secretary. "Make a note to ask the AA club to call on Sam."

There is an Alcoholics Anonymous club that meets at Wheat Street Baptist Church every Friday evening. Most of the parishioners don't even know of its existence.

"These are the finest people in the world," the pastor says. "With many, I've lived right through their experience. I know something of their initial struggle, of the turning to God for strength, of the reliance upon God and the fellowship of fellow sufferers to maintain personal discipline. We should tell the story of these people to the whole church, but they won't let me. They're wonderful people. They tolerate me, and they can do a lot for Sam if he will listen to them."

There seems to be in this church no end to needs, and no lack of imagination and desire to meet those needs.

5

Civil Rights

The Baptist World Alliance was scheduled to meet in Atlanta in 1939. Delegates from all over the world would be in attendance. Every day, as he entered or left his basement sanctuary and looked at the church's gaunt frame of steel, the partially erected stone and masonry walls, the Reverend William Holmes Borders felt sad. He did not want those Baptist delegates from all over the world to see an American Negro Baptist church mired down in despair and failure.

Acting on his own, he called in some building inspectors, who went over the church's existing structure. They studied the blueprints originally drawn by the architectural firm of Daniel Butell more than a dozen years before. The judgment was reassuring. The present structure was sound, the plans good, the design modern and practical. From a construction standpoint, there was no good reason for not completing the Wheat Street Baptist Church as originally conceived by its late pastor, the Reverend Peter James Bryant.

Still acting on his own, Borders went to the Citizens Trust Company of Atlanta and was assured of the necessary loan, estimated at $110,000. The pastor took the contractor to his Board of Deacons meeting. Between the pastor's enthusiasm and the contractor's assurance of completion before the Baptist World Alliance meeting, the Board of Deacons agreed. An affirmative church vote followed.

The pastor's enthusiasm for this project was contagious. He let it be known that Wheat Street Baptist Church was going to stand proud in the sun. Sunday by Sunday a willing congregation gave more and more to the building fund.

The interior furnishings were hardly in, the paint barely dry, on the new Wheat Street Baptist Church building, when the delegates to the World Baptist Alliance commenced arriving in Atlanta. Many African and Asian delegates visited this Negro church, and some came back several times. They talked with the pastor, the deacons, the church members. This building and the land on which it stood represented, in its two construction periods, an investment of approximately $500,000. That an American Negro congregation in the South could build such a church unaided was in considerable contrast to what many delegates had believed to be the slavelike existence of the southern Negro.

The completion of their church greatly lifted the spirits of the congregation. The initial enthusiasm did not diminish with the departure of the Baptist World Alliance delegates. In just three and a half years the indebtedness on the new church structure was paid off. A twenty-year-old dream had at last been realized.

Then came a crisis. Late in 1945, four Negroes, a man, a boy, and two girls, were lynched near Monroe, Georgia, not far from Atlanta. The news hit Atlanta's Negro quarters like a thunderbolt. The frightened pulled their shades and spoke in whispers, and others, of a more defiant breed, gathered at street corners and spoke loudly of revenge. The county sheriff said he had no leads. The Atlanta newspapers and the wire services prowled Monroe for story material, for the missing facts. No one would talk.

One of the lynch victims was a middle-aged farmhand, one who had been in the city jail. On the afternoon of the lynching, a white man paid the fine and took this Negro out of jail. They were getting into the white man's car, to drive out to the farm, when two girls and a young boy, who lived near the farm, asked for a ride. Later reports all indicated that these three youngsters were the unfortunate victims of a cruel set of circumstances. On a lonely back road a mob of hooded men surrounded the car and took the Negro. Apparently one of the children recognized someone in the mob. This sealed their doom. However, the driver of the car denied that he had any knowledge of the identities of those who committed the crime. He could not account for the lynch mob's knowing that his car would be on that lonely back road, at that particular time, waiting for the intended victim.

As early as the second day, the familiar pattern of the news reports advised the native Georgian Negro that nothing was going to happen to bring those guilty of this crime to trial unless outside pressures were brought to bear. Borders and several other community leaders called for a mass meeting in the Wheat Street Baptist Church. It was their belief that the church should take a lead in exerting moral pressure to see that justice was achieved.

That evening the church was packed. The overflow crowd blocked much of Auburn Avenue. People came from all over Atlanta and neighboring communities. Borders was elected chairman of a permanent Committee of Action, and E. M. Martin of the Atlanta Life Insurance Company was elected treasurer. The only positive step taken that evening was to raise enough money to bury the victims.

Next day Borders telephoned the undertaker at Monroe and told him that the committee he represented had raised sufficient money to pay the funeral expenses of the victims. He then got into his car and drove to Monroe.

Monroe was a sleepy little country town, with its several business establishments facing the courthouse and village square. When Borders arrived, there was no one on the streets or in the stores. Even the benches in the little park surrounding the courthouse were empty. The courthouse clock alone seemed impervious to the hushed atmosphere.

At the undertaker's establishment, Borders was shown the four victims. He selected coffins, paid the undertaker in cash, got a receipt, and asked to talk to the victims' families.

The undertaker rode with him to show him the way. There was no conversation with the families of any of the victims. The family members had cried themselves out, and in the place of tears their eyes showed only fear. Would four deaths be enough? If so many had been killed so senselessly, what would those responsible for the lynching do if they feared someone would talk? How many more deaths were possible in Monroe?

Fully aware of the cause of the fears of the families, Borders drove the undertaker back to his place of business.

That evening in Atlanta, before another equally large gathering at the church, he told of his day's experience in Monroe. While talking, he was called to the telephone. It was the undertaker from Monroe. The families of the victims wanted to thank him, and the people he represented, for arranging and paying for the funerals. However, the families had decided it would be better to have a Negro minister from a nearby community conduct the service. Therefore it would not be necessary for Borders to return.

The wire services and the Negro press in America carried the story of the protest committee meeting at the Wheat Street Baptist Church. From all over the United States money was sent to the committee, which was soon able to post a $5,000 reward for any information leading to an arrest and conviction. The state of Georgia offered another $5,000 reward.

The size of the rewards brought several detectives to Atlanta who were interested in working on the case. Most went home after talking to local authorities. One man, a white man, went to Monroe and stayed about three weeks.

On his way home, empty-handed, he stopped in Atlanta to see Borders, who had paid some of his expense money. "Reverend, you're not going to get a conviction unless somebody on the inside talks. Everybody in Monroe knows what happened, that it was planned, premeditated. It was done to silence the Negro who was jailed because he got drunk and had objected to a white man sleeping with his wife. And everyone knows that one of the girls recognized someone in the mob and called out his name. That meant curtains for the kids. The white folks know the story. The black folks know the story. Everyone knows that if anyone talks there will be more killings."

Several weeks later six members of the committee, including Borders, went to Monroe to see the sheriff.

There were people loitering on the park benches now. As soon as the car carrying the six "outside" Negroes stopped in front of the courthouse, the loiterers disappeared. Borders and his associates sat in the car and waited. In a few minutes the sheriff came out. He placed one foot on the running board and stooped over to talk to them. In seconds, as though they had popped up out of the ground, the car was surrounded by thirty or forty white men.

"What them niggers want, Sheriff?" someone asked.

"Just want to know what progress we making on them lynchings," the sheriff replied.

"Need any help, Sheriff?"

"Nope."

The mob drifted back slowly to the benches and watched the meeting.

The discussion with the sheriff lasted about thirty minutes. The sheriff told them Monroe was usually a nice, friendly, peaceful town. Everyone knew everyone else. The whites knew all the Negroes and the Negroes knew all the whites. To prove his point, he pointed to a rooster crossing the street and said it belonged to Aunt Becky, a Negro woman, and everyone in Monroe knew it was her rooster. Then the sheriff said he had not been able to find a single clue, that he had talked to everybody, but no one knew anything.

The committee group then drove back to Atlanta.

In September, 1945, the National Baptist Convention of the USA, Inc., then claiming to represent five million Negro Baptists, had voted to hold their next annual meeting in Atlanta. The wire services had hardly put out the story of the Monroe lynchings before the convention was under pressure to move its meeting away from the Georgia capital. Pressure came from all parts of the Negro community and from all parts of the country. Many ministers did not want to go to Atlanta. Many lay people favored a boycott of Georgia. As chairman of the committee that had successfully submitted Atlanta's bid as host city, Borders fought to retain the convention.

"There is all the more reason now for coming to Atlanta," he insisted. "We must let these people know that we will not be intimidated, and we must take this opportunity to present to the people of America a reasoned and intelligent petition for justice, justice for all Americans, regardless of their race, or that part of the country in which they reside. Furthermore, if this convention comes to Atlanta, I will organize and personally lead a pilgrimage of the delegates to the site of the lynching to register our protest in Monroe itself."

The convention came to Atlanta.

Meanwhile, the lynch committee had been kept busy. Word would come out of Monroe that the white power structure there had become suspicious of a Negro. When the committee would find this Negro, usually a boy in his late teens or early twenties, he would be so battered and beaten as to need hospitalization. In every instance the boy and his family had been threatened that if now, or later, they mentioned a word of what had happened in Monroe, the mob would come looking for both the victim of the beating and his family.

The Atlanta committee would take the victim to a hospital in the city. As soon as he was able to travel, the committee paid the boy's transportation to Cleveland, Ohio, or New York City. They also advanced some money to help the boys get started in these northern cities. In all, the committee brought nine such battered victims out of Monroe.

"Of course there was never an official report of what happened to the boys," Borders recalls. "We knew what had happened. Nor did we ask the boys to tell us about the lynchings. We knew the persons involved, the motives, but we lacked evidence, legal evidence. All those battered boys could have told us was mere hearsay evidence, and Georgia was not convicting any white man on a Negro's report of hearsay evidence. We got the boys out of Monroe, patched them up physically, and sent them off to the North with our prayers and some money. I don't believe one of those boys ever came back to Monroe."

The ninth and last victim of Monroe vengeance had just been sent North, after several weeks of convalescence in Atlanta, when more than five thousand delegates of the National Baptist Convention arrived in Atlanta.

As he had promised, Borders had completed arrangements for a pilgrimage of delegates to Monroe. Many of the delegates were afraid. With the other committee members at his side, Borders took the platform at the convention and pleaded for the success of this protest, a protest to Monroe, to the state of Georgia, and to the nation.

Most of the delegates still would not go. However, a caravan of nearly two hundred automobiles, each filled with Negro Baptist ministers, pulled away from Wheat Street Baptist Church on a warm September morning. Before entering the cars, there had been a word of prayer. The prayer that morning asked for a repentant heart of those responsible for the crime, asked the Lord's loving grace to comfort the families of the victims, and asked that those making this pilgrimage would have the courage to bear their grievances and shame with a forgiving heart.

Driving the cars were many of the Negro business leaders of Atlanta.

There was little conversation en route, for each man was deep in his own thoughts. Borders recalled words from a gospel hymn, "Lord, you've brought us a long, long ways!" Yes, but like the Israelites in the wilderness, he suddenly wanted to know how much longer. It was only eighty-odd years since his daddy, who was making the trip with him, had been born a slave. "Thank you, Lord, we've come a long, long way." But in his mind there lurked the question, How much longer?

The caravan of cars stirred up the sleeping dust of Monroe. The cars drove around the courthouse square, and then parked in solid phalanx before the courthouse. The local populace was startled. They had never before seen so many well-dressed Negro men riding in cars. The courthouse loiterers were sorely outnumbered.

Borders stepped from his car and stood waiting. Shortly the sheriff came out to meet him.

"What's this about, Reverend?" the sheriff asked. It was the first time the sheriff had ever addressed him as a minister.

"These are all Baptist ministers," he told the sheriff. "They are members of the National Baptist Convention of America. They represent over five million Negro Baptists. Their annual meeting is being held in Atlanta this week. These are just a few of the delegates attending. These ministers have come to see this Georgia town where four innocent people were lynched. They've come to see the house where the man lives who double-crossed the victims. They would like to see the double-crosser himself, if he has the nerve. They are going to visit that lonely spot on the back road where the mob lynched these poor souls. They are going to visit the graves of the victims. And they want to see the sheriff who has failed the victims and their families and the promises of justice for all which is the heritage of this country.

"They are here to protest what happened here. They want the people of Monroe to know that they, as Christians, think the crimes committed here will be judged before both God and man. They want the people of this great country to know that the Negro ministers of America protest the absolute breakdown of law and order as represented here by the failure of justice in Monroe, Georgia."

Borders had written out his brief statement in anticipation of such a confrontation. He had not wished to trust his words to the emotions of the moment. He had spoken loudly so that his words would carry to those in the cars, and also to those on the park benches. Now he looked up.

The sheriff stood red-faced. There was an uneasy moment. This elected official swept his angry gaze the length of the phalanx of cars. Then without a word he turned and walked back to the courthouse.

Borders got back in his car and led the pilgrimage caravan on the remainder of their rounds through the town of Monroe, Georgia.

6

The Lord's Business

A FEW YEARS later there was another senseless and brutal killing of Negroes, this time at Americus, Georgia. Known as the Ingraham case, it incited the Negro populace almost as much as had the lynchings at Monroe. C. A. Scott, publisher of the Atlanta *World*, and other Atlanta Negro leaders, begged the Reverend William Holmes Borders to again head a committee to seek justice for these people. He refused.

"I didn't believe I could win this case. Americus is in the southern part of Georgia. I had no roots there. After the experience at Monroe, it seemed unlikely that I could gain information in Americus to help these poor people. Nor did I want all that freedom money, from all over the country, coming in here. People who send freedom money have high hopes. I simply couldn't face the prospect of failing them.

"Perhaps without fully realizing it, I had made a major decision in my civil rights fight. I think that is when I made up my mind to do my civil rights fighting in my own home town, Atlanta. Here I know my people. Here I have contacts with the leaders of the other race. I am here all of the time. That means that if I start something, I am going to be here to finish it. I don't believe in starting something and not being around to finish it. It's how we finish the job that counts."

There were no other major civil rights atrocities in those years during the late fifties; just the hateful yoke of segregation's continuing economic slavery. Borders knew that his people were becoming increasingly restive. They often voiced open criticism of the mainstream of American life, which they saw as neither for nor against them. What could freedom and justice and democracy mean to this apathetic white majority of Americans who ignored the basic American principles of equal justice for all? More and more the critical voices of the Negro community picked up phrases from the radical fringes, always present, always waiting with a poisoned answer.

Borders countered these untruths with the Bible, with its promises of love, and his own assurance that a way for their redemption would be revealed.

There was genuine fear, almost terror, after the awesomeness of the H-bomb was revealed. The Negro community suddenly found itself perched on the brink of destruction, involved against its will by a world denied to the Negro. For many, the H-bomb did not speak of progress. To this sense of apprehension Borders spoke out from the pulpit.

"We are, in our world today, wandering on the brink of total disaster. A few bombs would destroy all of us. This total destructive ability has been brought about by a sophisticated culture long denied to the black man. We ask, 'Is this our struggle?' "

For an answer he quoted Psalm 37:1-3:

"Fret not thyself because of evildoers, neither be thou

envious against the workers of iniquity. For they shall soon be cut down like the grass, and wither as the green herb. Trust in the Lord, and do good; so shalt thou dwell in the land, and verily thou shalt be fed."

As the civil rights struggle enlarged and new organizations with new programs appeared in the Negro ghetto, as the old slums were being called, the competition for the average person's loyalty and support drastically increased. Everyone had his pick of programs, from violence to nonviolence, from street fights to court fights. It seemed to Borders to be a good time to preach a series of sermons about the children of Israel delivered out of Egypt. Again he turned to poetry, to the idiom of the Little Williams, to the man in the street, to describe the Bible's promise:

> The children of Israel were a lost and flung-down people.
> Away from home, down in the land of Egypt.
> Salt was sprinkled in the open wounds of these slaves,
> For they were hard pressed and driven like cattle.
> They moaned, and God heard their groans,
> For slavery hurt His heart.
> The Almighty dipped His pen in the ink of eternity
> And wrote Israel's Emancipation Proclamation.
>
> . . . .
>
> Israel got hungry. The angels cooked some manna,
> On the big gas range of glory.
> They dropped it down, properly seasoned and salted,
> Wrapped in heavenly packages.
> Israel got thirsty. Moses melted the rocks;
> A spring bubbled cool water.
> The children shouted around the spring,
> Some stooped down and lapped water.

These were troubled days. Through Borders' contacts with the other race, especially the political contacts at City Hall, he worked hard for his people. Of Mayor William B. Hartsfield, who had presided over the affairs of Atlanta for more than two decades, who had originally scoffed at the idea of Negro policemen, he said: "At first I thought the mayor was a segregationist. Later I discovered that he was a most practical politician. With him, you would always know what you had to deliver to get what you wanted. The man grew in office. He learned to work for all of Atlanta. He never broke his promises to me. When he agreed to do something, he worked as hard as you to see that it came off smoothly. I could do business with him."

Also, there was appearing in the South, and particularly in Atlanta, a new breed of white businessmen. For the most part they were young men, many with childhood roots in the South. For long years they had studied the economic ills of the South, troubled by its lagging business growth and economic stagnation. They had come to a realization that you cannot exclude, or hold down, the education and economic opportunities of much of the population—30, 40, or 50 percent—and expect business to grow. These men commenced speaking up to the mayor. They advised him that the white power structure of Atlanta had to include in its planning the welfare and needs of the entire city, regardless of race.

It now became much easier to talk to the mayor about equalization of salaries for Negro teachers, recreational and planned off-street programs for Negro youth, better health and sanitation facilities, the opening of jobs in the city to qualified Negroes. There was much more. Not everything was getting done at once, and the accomplishments never came fast enough. The important thing, however, was the fact that something was getting done. The lines of communication between the races were open. Tradition was no longer sacred. Progress was sought.

Borders and his wife had both given up their college teaching positions to concentrate their total effort in the church and neighborhood. Just as they seemed to be making headway, Borders' father died.

This was early in January, 1949. The family gathered from many parts of the nation, and the funeral was held at the Wheat Street Baptist Church. Then the family drove a hundred miles across the farmlands of Georgia from Atlanta to Macon. The elder Borders had asked to be carried back to Macon to lie at the side of his wife. This was done.

In recalling the funeral, Borders says: "I did not feel sad, nor shed a tear. I felt good inside. I knew that his physical departure was inevitable, and that I had done the best I could by him. I had paid the mortgage on the homestead, seen my younger brother through school, and with my wife had cared for his needs during those last years. My conscience was clear inside, but my poor wife did the crying. She had loved him very, very much. There were times when I was convinced that she loved him even better than I did.

"Later, when we sold the family homestead, I saw that each of my brothers and sisters (or if deceased, their spouse), received their share of the money. I knew this would satisfy my father's heart. It also satisfied my heart, because I was then, as now, guided by his great spirit.

"During one of my early years, I slept in the same room with him. My father always awakened at dawn. He prayed aloud and many times I heard him pray when he thought that I was asleep. I heard him pray for his children, one by one, and for himself, and for his church. I heard him ask God to reveal the text and subject for the following Sunday. All of these things got deeply rooted in me, and I never was able, and happily so, to rid myself of them completely. To be sure, I learned from many, many people—some illiterate persons in my church and some of the most hardened critics of this century. But, chiefly, I learned from my father. Even now, when I have complex problems which vex me mightily, I can feel the warmth of his spirit. His influence and guidance are still with me."

The parsonage seemed empty without the elder Borders, and especially so with the Borders' two children away at Charlotte Hawkins Brown's boarding school in North Carolina. This was the first year that the children had both been away, and Mrs. Borders seemed unable to focus her attention on her normal activities.

Borders remembered how once his wife had told him, "Nobody has ever bathed my children but me. And I have given them a bath every day of their lives."

As he watched her listlessness, he became worried.

On Easter Sunday, Mrs. Borders arose early, fried some chicken, cooked an entire meal, placed it in a portable warmer, and flew to North Carolina to see the children and to share this home-cooked meal with them. The children were surprised and all cried together. "This seemed to release my wife's tensions, and she became herself again, a fastidious person, a meticulous planner, a tireless worker."

That summer, true to her earlier promises, their daughter, Juel Pate Borders, worked with the deaf class and trained a widening number of new leaders. The son, William Holmes Borders, Jr., was active in the Gospel Chanters and the Sunday school, which Mrs. Borders directed in her capacity as Christian education director. Just as fast as Mrs. Borders could train Sunday-school teachers, the classes filled up. Wheat Street Baptist Church was about to pop its seams.

As he labored in the Lord's vineyard, Borders dreamed of

his son following in the ministry, preparing himself to take over Wheat Street Baptist Church. One day Billy revealed other plans: "Daddy, I don't want to be a preacher. I'm going to be a doctor."

Later the son graduated from medical school at Howard University, Washington, D.C., while the daughter earned her medical degree at the Woman's Medical College of Pennsylvania, Philadelphia. "They're my kids," Borders says, "and I'm proud of them. I helped them through medical school and I've helped them set up their practice here in Atlanta. They are both active in Wheat Street Church. But I don't deny there is a disappointment. At first it was keen. It left me prone to self-pity, probably the meanest and most devastating of all human emotions. I think my wife realized my problem, so she tossed me a great big problem to solve."

The problem was the simple fact that the Sunday-school department had outgrown the church basement. It needed two or three times more classroom space. Mrs. Borders stated the problem quite tersely: "Wheat Street Baptist Church needs a Christian Education Building."

"We can't spend all that money just for Sunday-school classrooms," he protested.

"I know that," she replied. "So we're organizing a day-school nursery program, to operate five days a week. Holmes, Wheat Street has a number of families where both parents work, and these preschool children are not receiving proper care. The baby-sitters are old folks who raised their children on a farm, and just can't seem to adapt to the changes urban living demands when raising children. And what do our old-timers know about balanced diets, proper rest, cleanliness? Holmes, you come with me. I'll show you. Being a man, you probably don't even know that our Negro infant mortality rate is nearly double that of the other race."

After a day's visitation, Borders had no argument left. A Christian Education Building for the Sunday school on Sunday, for the day-care nursery school during the week, for the church bodies and auxiliary meetings during the evenings, was the next part of the Wheat Street story.

The plan was announced to the Board of Deacons and to the church, and then this $400,000 project was under way.

While his wife made lists of needed equipment, sought advice and assistance of state regulating agencies, and compiled lists of trained nurses, teachers, dietitians, and other helpers, he went to City Hall.

Directly across from the church, facing on Fort Street, was a 200-by-200-foot plot of ground on which there were seven houses. They were jammed together and so dilapidated that they had the appearance of leaning against each other to keep from falling down.

Through political contacts at City Hall, Borders discovered the owner, and was able to purchase the property at a reasonable price. Then came the heartbreaking task of finding housing for the present occupants.

The church promised these people free rent until other suitable housing was located. As bad as the old housing had been there by the church, it took two months to find other quarters that these people could afford to rent. In only one instance, and here the man had a little money of his own, was the new housing an improvement.

"Sometimes you live right on top of a problem, you talk about it, but it is not a vital part of you," the pastor observed. "I had grown up in houses like that. The sight of them didn't shock me. I called for new housing, I spoke of new housing, but not until that incident did I speak in terms of the suffering of people. I had had my eyes opened."

A friend at City Hall told Borders that the property directly in back of the church on Fort Street was part of an estate and would be sold by sealed bids. Borders placed a bid and shortly was advised that the church had its second site for the Christian Education Building.

Opinion was unanimous that the second site would be better for the building. After the land was cleared and graded, the original site was fenced in and converted to a playground during the week and an off-street parking lot on Sunday.

On May 7, 1957, the Christian Education Building was dedicated. A two-story brick building, it has fourteen classrooms, two offices, a complete kitchen, and a large multipurpose room that serves as Sunday dining room, Sunday-school assembly room, and day-school gymnasium. The most modern equipment was placed in the classrooms, which were properly equipped for the small children. The adult and teen-age classes continued to meet in the church basement, but the Sunday-school children's department and the new Wheat Street Day Nursery School had new accommodations. There were no finer classrooms in Atlanta.

Right from the start the day-school program was overcrowded. The enrollment was stopped at one hundred until staff and state licensing agencies agreed that the staff had the experience to accept more pupils. These are from age two through five. Parents pay one dollar a day, regardless of the number of children attending from one family. The church purchased six buses; they pick up the children and take them to school, where they are supervised, fed, take naps, play with each other, and are taught. The program operates from 7 A.M. until 5 P.M. The entire program has been approved by state and city regulatory agencies and is conducted by registered teachers and nurses.

From the inception of the Day Nursery School program,

and more recently with the addition of the church's Project Headstart summertime program, the two Borders children have contributed topflight medical assistance without charge. Probably no other group of children in Atlanta have such complete medical and dental diagnosis and care, with much of the latter contributed gratis because of the recipient families' inability to pay.

In part, this medical program stems from a considerable sacrifice made by Borders and his wife. Their children both married before finishing medical school, and each soon had a family. When both children decided to take graduate studies in their specialized fields, their respective spouses had to take jobs to help meet educational and living expenses. This meant that four grandchildren had to be cared for, and Borders and his wife took on this arduous responsibility.

They brought the grandchildren from Philadelphia and Washington, D.C., and soon the parsonage home in Atlanta had a young-family look and activity.

Borders recalls their initial adjustments to this change. "My wife told me that caring for the grandchildren, especially at her age, would shorten her life. She said she was willing to take this responsibility in order that her children might perfect themselves in their respective medical specialties. She wanted our children to have every opportunity to succeed. She knew, and I knew, the sacrifice she was making.

"We took our four grandchildren willingly. I did the shopping and scrubbing. However, the major tasks fell upon my wife. She took the responsibility for the preparation of the food, for guidance, for the teaching of prayers at night, for the teaching of rhymes, for teaching, teaching, teaching. She selected their television programs, read to them, took them on tours. The major portion of the Christian education was upon her shoulders. She did a remarkable job. We had gained wisdom and experience from raising our own family. Perhaps this led her to do an even better job with our grandchildren.

"To me it was very sweet to watch my wife's love and devotion to our grandchildren. Never across the flight of eternity's years shall I escape the emotional and binding love shown in her sacrifice."

When the Borders' children finished their medical studies and returned to Atlanta, establishing their own homes, Mrs. Borders had to face the return of her charges to their parents. Rather than weep through the children's departure, she took a sudden trip to visit a friend in a distant city.

Dr. William Holmes Borders, Jr., specialized in internal medicine and Dr. Juel Pate Borders Benson specialized in obstetrics and gynecology. Juel married Dr. Theodore Benson, a dentist. This family trio comprises a rather complete set of medical-dental specialists for the church's educational programs.

It was the completion of the Christian Education Building which made possible the church's neighborhood educational services. After the completion of this building, which the church paid for in three years, the members of the Wheat Street Baptist Church gave their pastor and his wife a round-the-world trip. This was an expression of the church's appreciation for more than twenty years of leadership, fruitful years of change which had always found the pastor able to meet the church's growing needs.

At first Borders had protested. He had other ways to spend that money. However, his wife calmed him down.

"Holmes, our people know they'll never make such a trip themselves. Now you came right out of the same red gumbo

Georgia clay that most of them did. You'll be making this trip for them. Besides, Holmes, it will enable us to visit the Holy Land."

The trip had been a rest, a blessing. Borders' tired spirits had been renewed as he trod the sands of the Holy Land. In India, the character and depths of the man Gandhi, revealed through story and writing, had captivated him. And there had been even moments of sheer relaxation. One such moment had been a fiery sunset beside the island-dotted Aegean Sea. They watched the sun's yellow afterglow, brushing the summits of the rocky Greek islands, and then fade into the purples of the evening. From memory each quoted parts of Homer's epic poetry. For a moment it seemed like being back at the seminary and college, detached from the struggles of man, mindful only of the joy of pure learning for the sake of learning. They surprised themselves by the amount of poetry they remembered. They reveled in the experience. It so captured their thoughts that neither would have been surprised if the long dark hull of Odysseus' ship had skimmed out across those waters as that intrepid sailor searched for the illusive port called home.

Ever since, both of them referred to this experience as their honeymoon.

Since their return to Atlanta there had been no time for relaxation. The civil rights pace had quickened. There were new organizations seeking Borders' support. He was a lifetime member of N.A.A.C.P., but now other groups were asking him to speak around the country. He had personal friends in every organization. They all sought the same goals. As an individual, however, he could not participate in his intense, active way in every organization. He needed guidance through these new waters. So he had gone back to Swift Creek Baptist Church, and there had prayed to the Lord.

The next day, back at the Wheat Street Baptist Church, a Mrs. Edna Fulton, a member of the church whom he did not personally know, came to call on him. She was in tears, she was in trouble, and she needed help.

Mrs. Fulton was a large woman, poor and weary. She was a scrubwoman. She had two jobs, cleaning a number of private homes during the day and an office building at night. She put in over fourteen hours work a day and yet her two jobs paid her but fifty dollars a week.

She had needed some medical attention and her son's family had needed some help. Mrs. Fulton had borrowed three hundred dollars without understanding the contract she signed. She had been paying on this debt for over two years. She had never missed a payment, yet the principal had hardly been reduced. She had reached the point where she had no place to turn and she was too weary to go on.

"Preacher," she implored, "can't you pay my debt? Can't some of the good Christian folk of this church pay my debt? I will pay you back. I just can't pay all that interest."

Borders called an attorney, a member of the church who was well respected at City Hall. The attorney agreed to take Mrs. Fulton's case, which was shortly settled out of court on the basis of what she had already paid.

"That woman's plight started me thinking," Borders recalls. "There was no question that the folks right here in this church had needs, serious needs, that weren't being met. If I went running around the country speaking about civil rights, about lifting up our people, of providing them rightful freedoms and opportunities, what would happen to my people at home? Wasn't civil rights something to demonstrate, to prove, in one area and spread to other areas? I still don't know the answer to that one, except insofar as it applies to me.

This is the way I work best, and it is the course I realized the Lord intended for me to follow. I had the Mrs. Fultons to take care of, to think about, to plan for, and if someone like this couldn't turn to her church in her need and desperation, where could she go?"

Borders talked to some bankers, did some reading at the public library, and soon had a plan. He talked his idea over with the attorney who handled Mrs. Fulton's case. With acquaintances at City Hall he talked about the peculiar needs of the people of Wheat Street Baptist Church. He didn't stop talking until he was certain that what the church needed was a credit union.

One night, after a church meeting, he got some people together and told them of his plan. Nine people put in five dollars apiece. With this $45 investment the Wheat Street Baptist Church Credit Union was started. The number of savers has grown from nine to over six hundred, and the amount on deposit has increased from $45 to over $200,000. However, the growth did not come without planning and work and prayer.

Borders became increasingly aware of how often Jesus spoke of the matter of finances: "Where your treasure is, there will your heart be also" (Matt. 6:21).

For the next few Sundays the sermons at Wheat Street Baptist Church became a strange mixture of gospel passages dealing with stewardship and the practical knowledge of the difference between simple and compound interest.

Then he announced that there was now a Wheat Street Baptist Church Credit Union. Its purpose was to teach and encourage thrift. It would provide interest on the members' deposits. Officers of the credit union would give the members counsel on matters of finances, and when someone had valid needs for money, they would loan the money at the lowest possible interest rates.

Never bashful, he announced: "Old ladies, I want your snuff money. Men, I want your cigarette money. Kids, I want your ice-cream money. I don't care if all you can set aside each week is a quarter. If that's all you can save, then save that quarter. But save it. Save it each week. Your credit union office will be open for an hour each Sunday after the preaching service."

Teaching thrift to people who live in the slums, in an area identified by the government as "disadvantaged" and needy, is not easy. "Instead of six hundred savers, we should have twenty-six hundred," says Borders. "You don't wait until you have more money than you can spend before you start to save. Someone has to teach this to our people. We're making progress. Our number of deposits has doubled in the past two years. The amount on deposit has multiplied five or six times in that period of time. More of our people are catching the spirit and purpose of savings. They are finding satisfaction and peace of mind in the security of savings.

"Our credit union is paying one-half percent more interest than the commercial savings associations. The people who run our credit union are not highly trained. Most have no education beyond high school. They are sincere people. They work hard, they work long hours, and they work without pay. They know our people. They know our neighborhood and this community. They make few mistakes. Most important, they know they are filling a real need for the people of this church. Their reward is the pride and joy of serving. Their example and their accomplishments are a source of inspiration to the entire membership of the Wheat Street Baptist Church. And I marvel at what has happened to the lives of these officials. The responsibility and discipline of their voluntary job has shown them inner strengths that they didn't know they had. This has provided them with incentives and vision much broader than themselves. This growth has been a joy to see."

7

The Bus Strike

In no part of the country have poverty and ignorance, those twin destroyers of freedom, so shackled the Negro as in Alabama and Mississippi. If conditions are bad for the Negro in Georgia, he takes comfort in the knowledge that life in Alabama or Mississippi would probably be worse.

Negroes often tell one another stories that take their humor from a bitter edge of truth. Such a sardonic story spread through Atlanta a few years ago. It told of the Negro GI who became separated from his unit while on field maneuvers in Alabama. Seeking to rejoin his command, the soldier crawled through the underbrush. He suddenly came face to face with a poisonous snake. The soldier aimed his gun at the snake. "Don't shoot! Don't shoot!" cried the snake. "I'm trying to get out of Alabama too."

Obviously the Negro expects few results from civil rights demonstrations in these two states, and when any major civil rights step is initiated there, that is indeed news.

Such was the case in the hard-fought, bitterly contested Montgomery bus strike. News of the strike in the Alabama city was a major topic in the Negro slums everywhere, and as the bus strike evolved into a legal battle and headed for the United States Supreme Court, interest and hopes mounted. Not since the Supreme Court's public school desegregation decision in 1954 had that judicial body dealt with a case of such far-reaching importance to the Negro community. To desegregate the buses would mark the breaking of one more of those hateful shackles of the slave-servant relationship. One more of those humiliating and denigrating practices which spoke of substandard citizenship and provoked self-hatred would have been torn away.

When the United States Supreme Court decision desegregating the buses in Montgomery was announced, the Negroes of America greeted the news joyfully. Another fetter binding them to an unhappy past had been destroyed.

In Atlanta, the Reverend William Holmes Borders and several other Negro leaders with ready access to City Hall lost no time in letting it be known that the Negro people of Atlanta wanted that city's buses desegregated. At that time there was in Georgia, as had been the case in Alabama, a state law prohibiting this.

It soon became apparent that city officials were dragging their feet. Even in progressive Atlanta, where businessmen and politicians had vowed that the white power structure must give more than lip service to the Negro populace and its rightful needs and aspirations, there was uneasiness. Although Atlanta is the hub of Georgia, and increasingly enlightened in official attitude, much of the remainder of the state is rural and bound to past concepts of segregation. The political fortunes in the state have, for a number of years, wavered like a teeter-totter between liberal and conservative ideas.

At that particular time the state offices were under the control of Governor Marvin Griffin, a segregationist in every traditional sense of the word. The city officials and the Negro ministers had no desire to tip their hand to the governor's heavy-handed policemen and prosecutors.

Knowing that their people would not wait longer and should not, the Negro pastors of Atlanta met and organized the Triple L movement. The three "L's" stood for "love, liberty, and loyalty." The announced purpose of this Triple L movement was to desegregate the buses of the Atlanta Transit Company. Borders was elected chairman of the group.

Ordinarily the committee met during the daytime. Each evening these ministers addressed church gatherings, informing their people of what the Triple L movement was going to do and what they, the people, were not to do. The movement's governing body had, with legal advice, determined to have a test case, a deliberate violation of the Georgia law, followed by contest of the continued enforcement of the law through court action. They did not want mass uprisings, civil disobedience, or marches. It was all to be done as simply as possible, without inciting either race.

The time for action arrived. The Triple L committee advised Mayor William B. Hartsfield, all the Atlanta aldermen, Chief of Police Herbert Jenkins, and the Atlanta Transit Company that they were going to challenge the Georgia law of segregation on common carriers.

The mayor stated that he would not recommend such action. Local newspapers were filled with stories of impending trouble on the buses.

Borders and the other pastors who were identified with the Triple L movement received threatening telephone calls. They were subjected to personal invective, to threats of bodily harm for themselves and for their families. Several threats were also made to dynamite the Wheat Street Baptist Church.

On the Sunday before the impending violation of the law, Borders preached to a packed congregation. He had a rather awkward title to his sermon, "God told Moses, Go down and tell ole Pharaoh to set my people free."

On the morning of January 9, 1957, acting as chairman of the Triple L movement, Borders telephoned the mayor and told him that at ten thirty, in the heart of Atlanta, he and five other local Negro ministers would board an Atlanta Transit Company bus. Their purpose would be to sit in the front of the bus, whatever happened. The mayor tried to discourage such a step. Borders replied that the committee was going ahead anyway. He advised that at the request of their attorneys they were asking the city for full police protection in conformity with the basic spirit and intent of the Supreme Court's decision on the Montgomery bus strike case. The mayor, and later the chief of police, assured the committee that there would be no violence.

At ten thirty, at the busy Five Points intersection in the heart of Atlanta, Borders and five other Negro ministers boarded a city bus. After paying their fare, they took seats in the front of the bus in violation of the Georgia state law and practices of the Atlanta Transit Company.

They sat still, silent, staring ahead. A century of shame was being weighed, judged.

The bus driver said nothing. There was no incident. Several people of both races, seeing what was happening, got off the bus or failed to get on.

The bus pulled out and started its journey across town. The ministers rode the bus for four round trips before getting off. There were no arrests. In effect, nothing happened.

The committee decided that the city's official strategy was

to avoid arrest and incident, in the hope that the problem would go away. From Wheat Street Baptist Church Borders then telephoned the mayor and the chief of police. He told both men that he and the committee of the Triple L movement would be on the buses next day, and every day thereafter, until the city of Atlanta enforced the Georgia law governing segregation on common carriers.

The mayor called back shortly and said warrants were being sworn out for the arrest of the six Negro ministers. He asked if they wished to be arrested on that day's violations or preferred to stage another violation next day. The latter course was agreed to, on advice of their attorneys. Arrangements were then worked out as to the time of the bus violation incident and place of arrest. The mayor asked if he might send city limousines to take the ministers to City Hall, where they would be booked pending release on bond. The ministers said that they would ride to City Hall in the customary police paddy wagon.

Next afternoon the six ministers boarded a city bus, made one round trip, and as the bus returned to the heart of the city, dismounted in front of the Wheat Street Baptist Church. Negroes in the street cheered.

The ministers went inside the church. The huge sanctuary was partially darkened by late-afternoon shadows. The ministers sat quietly, praying. Within fifteen minutes the police arrived. Two police officers entered the church and politely informed the ministers that they had warrants for their arrest. They were charged with violation of the Georgia state law requiring segregation on common carriers. The officers asked the ministers to accompany them to City Hall. The ministers then walked out of the church with the police officers. With Borders were R. Williams, B. J. Johnson, Howard Bussy, Howard Fisher, and B. J. Short.

News that the six bus-riding ministers were back at the Wheat Street Baptist Church had spread throughout the Auburn Avenue business district. A radio station broadcast news flashes that the police paddy wagon had reached the church. When the officers and ministers emerged from the church building, they found the streets of the neighborhood completely blocked by a milling, shouting, carnival-spirited mob.

"The people knew why we were there, why the police were there," Borders recalled. "This was visible evidence, exciting evidence, that the test case against segregation on the buses of Atlanta was progressing as we had advised that it would. People quit work. They stopped cooking meals. They left beauty shops. They came out of stores. They thronged the streets. People even came over from the west side of Atlanta, a distance of five miles from the Wheat Street Church."

The paddy wagon was driven by a well-groomed and neatly dressed Negro policeman, one of the first of his race to have been hired by the Atlanta Police Department. As the ministers emerged from the church and walked through the happy crowd of cheering people, the Negro patrolman stepped smartly to the back of the paddy wagon, threw open its doors and said, "Step right in, gentlemen."

The ministers got into the paddy wagon while the happy crowd milled around. The officers got back into the front of the conveyance and started the motor. However, the people would not move. At times the crowd literally lifted the box-like paddy wagon off the pavement. The ministers were in danger of having the vehicle tipped over by their friends.

"There was absolutely no violence," Borders said. "These people were just excited, just so happy at the promised outcome of our actions that they had to pop off some steam."

Since the police were helpless to disperse the mob and move

the paddy wagon, Borders spoke to the police officers in the front. One of them got out, unlocked the barred double door at the back, and opened it. Standing on the steps where everyone could see him, Borders thanked the crowd for their support. "You've given us real joy. We are strengthened in the knowledge you are with us, are supporting us, in this bus strike. There is, however, nothing more that you can do. We must go through with this arrest so that this injustice can be met and dealt with properly in the courts of this country, by attorneys. Thank you for coming. Now please go home. Pray for our success. But right now, let us be arrested as we have planned."

The crowd cheered. Slowly the vehicle inched along as a path opened. From inside the swinging open doors at the rear of the wagon Borders and his fellow ministers waved to the crowd which, in turn, cheered and cheered.

At City Hall the six ministers were fingerprinted, questioned, charged, and jailed until they could be brought before a magistrate and released on bail. In all, they remained in jail about six hours. While incarcerated they utilized the time to sing and pray, much as the Bible tells us Paul and Silas did while imprisoned at Philippi.

Borders describes the experience with a smile. "We were treated throughout these happenings as though we were human beings. Of course this is how we should have been treated. However, under similar circumstances elsewhere, Negroes have been mistreated. Atlanta is wonderful—not perfect, but moving in the right direction. There are some of the best people on earth in Atlanta, white and Negro, and they know how to work together. They seek to prevent the rabble-rousers from taking over a situation. They try to do what is right for all of the people of Atlanta."

Later that night the attorneys posted bond and the six ministers were released. However, the governor, on being informed that Negroes were trying to ride in the front of the bus, placed the state militia on a standby alert.

Then followed an intolerable period of waiting. By prior agreement, the case had been filed in both state and federal courts. The problem was that of trying to clear the court dockets and give this case a quick hearing. During this waiting period, extreme elements of both races worked away at the fringes of public opinion. Borders and the other ministers representing the Triple L movement were frequently invited to share their opinions on radio and television programs.

During one program Borders was asked if any in the Negro community were afraid of negative reactions as a result of this Atlanta bus protest. He replied: "One of my friends, not one of my fellow ministers, went home the other night. When he got out of his car, a dog overturned the garbage can. This man grabbed his pistol. 'Look out, dog, you almost got shot.' "

Another question, one frequently asked, was why he got involved in the bus strike, since he had a car of his own and did not need to ride the bus.

He replied: "In the first place, I do ride the bus. I can't always find a parking place in downtown Atlanta. But even if I did not ride the bus, I would do what I am doing. This is not a question of mine or any other person's convenience. It is a question of what is morally right and just, and it is a question which involves a good many Americans with skin the color of mine, who wish to be treated like full-fledged Americans. This bus strike is one more step toward freedom for the American Negro."

On his own radio program Borders further clarified this viewpoint. "You must recall," he pointed out, "that there were Negroes, for reasons of their own, who were not with our movement. These Negroes informed city, county, and state officials that they were not with us. Remember also that the governor of Georgia threatened to call out the National Guard to enforce Georgia's state law of segregation on common carriers. Remember that we had every reason to expect vigorous and hostile opposition from some segments of the white populace. So we had to believe quite firmly, we had to have faith, that we are right in our stand, that we are helping our people and our city, in order to do what we have done. However, I would say our greatest surprise, our keenest disappointment, has been the attitude of some members of our own race."

The nature of this minority Negro opposition centered around unspoken insinuations. It was pointed out that the governing body of the Triple L movement were all leading Negro pastors. By Negro standards, all were well to do, owners of automobiles. Why did they lead the city bus strike? What was their interest? What would they, personally, get out of this?

Speaking again on the radio, Borders stated:

"President Franklin D. Roosevelt lived comfortably at Hyde Park, Warm Springs, and the White House; but he was the main instrument in getting public housing projects started all over America so that people might be warm. Wilberforce was never a slave, but he fought slavery for forty years. Lord Salisbury was not a chimney sweep or a child laborer, but he spearheaded laws against child labor and laws providing benefits for chimney sweeps. Lincoln was never sold on an auction block, but he wrote the Emancipation Proclamation which set the black man free. Jesus was never a sinner, but Paul said Jesus took upon himself the form of a servant and even death on the Cross that men through him might be saved. I do ride the bus. But if I did not, I would still prefer to walk the path of Roosevelt, Wilberforce, Salisbury, Lincoln, and Jesus. This in spite of any opposition."

In due time the courts heard the case, upheld the bus protest, which meant the Georgia state law of segregation on common carriers was unconstitutional.

Borders was at the church when the news reached him. He went into the sanctuary and prayed. His secretary told him a man kept calling on the telephone and asking for "that damned bus preacher." He told his secretary to tell the man that the Reverend William Holmes Borders was not available. On his knees he prayed.

His secretary returned to say that Mayor William B. Hartsfield of Atlanta was on the telephone. The mayor told him that he was taking steps to see that the desegregation of the city buses in Atlanta proceeded peacefully, without incident, and in the best interests of all the citizens of Atlanta. He requested the presence of Borders and his committee of ministers immediately at City Hall.

"This mayor was a practical politician," Borders said. "The courts had ruled. He quickly organized his forces and ours to implement that decision and to implement it in the most logical and orderly fashion possible."

The mayor assigned the Atlanta Transit Company the responsibility of immediately printing a hundred thousand circulars for distribution to bus riders, advising them of the court decision invalidating the old law, and explaining how people of both races were to behave. The mayor asked his public relations personnel to work with the Triple L committee members to prepare a special set of circulars to be distributed throughout the Negro community. These called on the Negro populace to prove to both races, both inside and outside Atlanta, that the changing of old segregation customs marked a step of progress and harmony in race relations, not retrogression. This statement was signed by the committee of ministers.

The mayor then telephoned to radio and television stations and got immediate time on the air. The mayor, the aldermen, the six ministers of the Triple L movement, and the chief of police spoke far into the night, addressing their remarks to all citizens of Atlanta, imploring an orderly, mannerly integration of the city buses next day. Their remarks were taped and played over and over again. The ministers called on their people to accept their victory with Christian charity in their hearts. "Be kind. Be polite. Sit wherever you wish. Behave in a manner which will bring credit to you as a person and to your race. People across the nation are looking at Atlanta to see if both races have matured, have grown up enough to take this step in harmony, without bloodshed, without incident."

"We worked all that night and far into the next day," Borders said. "The people of Atlanta were wonderful. The bus people were tremendous. We spoke to the bus drivers. The city officials were sincerely determined that there would be no incidents. And there were no incidents. Nobody wanted trouble. Everyone worked together to make this new freedom work. And it did work. The timing, the support, the procedures, all worked together in perfect unison, which happens when both races work together."

After the bus strike and aided by the election of a progressive governor in the state, the desegregation of other facilities in Atlanta progressed rapidly. In the area of restaurants there was the most opposition. The Student Non-Intervention Committee led the sit-in demonstrations.

Borders did not parade or sit-in. "I worked behind the scenes," he said. "I raised funds. I lectured to the marchers on the meaning of nonviolence as practiced by Gandhi.

"After the bus strike, the power structure here in Atlanta

did a job of preparing business and people for the desegregation of hotels, motels, restaurants, and other public facilities. There was some opposition, but for the most part these were isolated and represented individual actions. In the main, Atlanta integrated quickly, without major incident. Today, my people can eat and stay in whatever public facilities they choose in Atlanta.

"Every day some improvements in civil rights are made in Atlanta," Borders continued. "This is an upward drive. It is a matter of keeping a vigilant and constant pressure at those points where pressure is needed. It is being personally ready for improvements, for new opportunities, so that we don't muff the ball when new avenues are open to us. This is especially true in the field of economic opportunities. We must train and prepare ourselves better for jobs in business.

"Here in Atlanta we have made progress. We have excellent relations between the races. But outside of Atlanta, outside of Fulton County, much work needs to be done. The Negroes of Atlanta can help our brothers by providing money, leadership, assistance, public relations, legal counsel, and advice. However, I am a firm believer that all of this must be channeled through local organizations who represent the local Negro populace. They will have thought through their local problems, they will have endeavored to open lines of communication between the races at the local governmental levels, and they will be there to lead their people in proper utilization of their freedoms. Atlanta can help all of Georgia, all of the South."

8

Failure

In 1959 the Reverend William Holmes Borders persuaded the Wheat Street Baptist Church to purchase a 287-acre farm twenty-two miles from Atlanta. He had searched long and diligently for what he considered to be the right piece of property, but there were those church members who reacted quite negatively to the purchase. In the minds of these members, rural Georgia spoke of past bitterness, of intolerable conditions, of hunger and privation, of hatreds and prejudices. They predicted failure of the pastor's newest plan for the church.

Being fully aware of such feelings, the pastor had not discussed his plan with the church right away. He had gone to a real estate man, Ben Hurt, a member of the Wheat Street Baptist Church. Through Hurt's efforts he had looked at more than a dozen pieces of property before finding just the right one.

Borders wanted the property to be located on a well-traveled highway, and not more than twenty-five miles from Atlanta. The land had to have a running stream on it. Also, the property had to be entirely surrounded by white people.

"I had studied how rural property increases in value," he explained. "I knew that such improvements as electricity, gas, paved highways—all of which tend to increase property values —follow the main highways out of cities such as Atlanta. Also, I knew the South well enough to realize that when such advantages did penetrate into a rural area, they would first be offered to the white areas. I wanted to be in such an area. Now I always regard myself as a steward of the Lord's moneys, and I wanted any church property to increase in value, to get such improvements.

"To be right pointed, we paid forty-five thousand dollars for the farm, and I did not want to risk that much of the Lord's tithe money without reasonable expectation that the investment would pay for itself, whether or not my dream project materialized."

The dream project was one which must be familiar to every worker with the youth of city slums. "I wanted this farm for outdoor activities for boys. In the immediate vicinity of our church there are a large number of boys who need direction and care. There are pressures upon a boy in a slum. He is never really alone, never really has a quiet moment. Regardless of how he feels inside, he must display a bold public face. For most boys this results in a tough-guy attitude. I've actually had some boys tell me privately, 'Preacher, I ain't really tough. I'm just scared. But if I don't act tough, the other guys will know I'm scared. Then they really will clobber me.' "

In the neighborhood of the church there were boys too old for day nursery, who were accustomed to being in school nine months of the year. During the summer months they suddenly found themselves free of all supervision if both parents worked. Home alone, on their own, without proper food, without organized recreation to occupy them, such boys got into trouble. Often it isn't really the boys' fault, but the courts cannot always overlook the nature of the crime.

"We have this community problem each summer," Borders explained. "So I thought we could take these boys who needed direction and care to the farm of a summer. We could keep them there during the week, and bring them back over the weekend. We could raise cattle, and cut hay, and saw pulpwood, and raise pigs and chickens on the farm. We could plant gardens and grow vegetables.

"Do you know that we have boys, I have them right here in this church, who have never seen a live snake or a live rabbit? There may even be some who have never seen a cow—I don't know.

"I wanted these boys to have this outdoor experience. I wanted an opportunity to work with these boys, to lift their sights, to permit them the joy of quiet meditation in God's out-of-doors. Without the pressures of the city, I hoped that these boys would accept individual guidance."

Almost from the start this project brought unforeseen pressures to bear on Borders. The first were those within the church. Some members so hated their past lives in rural Georgia that they could not see any good being realized from such a project.

To cope with them, the pastor waited until the property was purchased. Then he announced to the church that they owned 287 acres of the finest land in Georgia, just twenty-two miles from Atlanta. He pointed out that if permitted to grow up in hay, the property would pay for itself. Besides, there was plenty of pulpwood in the wooded sections to recover the initial costs.

These people listened. They agreed to the potential of the

land, but they did not believe the church would ever be permitted to realize financial returns from the land. As one south Georgia native said, "Them red-gallused farmers don't want to pay a black man more than a no-good shack and a dollar a day. Well, they aren't going to stand by and see Negroes buy good property and make it pay. You wait and see."

An intermediary had been used by the real estate agent, himself a Negro, when the property was purchased. Now that the deed was recorded and the title to the land registered in the name of the church, Borders called on the neighbors.

"We had white neighbors on all sides of us. I talked to them about farming, about raising hogs and cattle, and selling pulpwood and cutting hay. I told them of my plan to bring our boys from the streets of Atlanta to summer on that farm. I promised that any new buildings would be placed back in the woods, off the highway, not just because they asked it, but because I wanted those boys to have a chance to get closer to the silence of the country, to be separated from all but the rustic atmosphere.

"These white neighbors acted right friendly. We seemed to maintain a surface form of civility. They told me who to see to get certain work done. The stores in the village didn't hesitate to sell us anything; some even offered credit."

Unknown to Borders, the second pressure was building up. His white neighbors were determined that no Negro—even a Negro church—would own property in their midst. The preacher's plan for a summer camp for boys from the slums of Atlanta was the final insult to them. They set about to make changes."

The Wheat Street Baptist Church held several picnics at the farm without incident. The pastor's plan seemed to be making progress.

The first sign of trouble arrived in the form of a committee of three of their new neighbors. The committee said they were prepared to buy the farm, and would pay what the church had paid for the property plus a fair value on the improvements.

Borders told them the farm was not for sale.

Monthly thereafter a delegation of white neighbors called at the church. Seldom were they the same people. As the months dragged on, the offer was gradually increased. As this happened, the pretended cordiality disappeared.

One morning Borders was summoned to the telephone. The call was from the little village near the farm. The farmhouse was on fire. He assured his caller that he would pay the $100 charge for the village fire department to make a call outside the village limits.

The fire department did go to the farm. However, by the time the fire equipment arrived, there was nothing to be done. The building had burned to the ground. The fire department submitted their bill for $100 for services rendered and the bill was paid.

The local sheriff reported the fire as one of "undetermined origin," and closed the case. There was never so much as a hearing and the pastor never saw a report of the findings.

In Borders' mind there grew an uneasy feeling that this was not entirely dissimilar to certain attitudes encountered over a decade before at Monroe, Georgia.

Several weeks after the fire, one of the church members who had most vigorously opposed purchase, and later retention, of the farm, called on Borders. He presented the pastor with a check for $8,000 made out to the church. So positive had this man been that the reaction of their white neighbors would be to burn them out that he had taken out an insurance policy on the farm buildings and had personally paid the premium.

This $8,000 and $2,500 realized from the sale of pulpwood brought the amount of the church's investment down to $34,500.

Following the fire, the buyers' committee of "our good neighbors," as Borders now called the white farmers, stopped calling personally at the church.

Instead, they went to State Senator LeRoy Johnson, a member of the Wheat Street Baptist Church and the first Negro to be elected to the Georgia State Senate in modern times. Senator Johnson was approached at the State Capitol by a man who said he had been authorized by the banker in the little village by the farm to offer "the Negro preacher" $300 an acre for the farm.

Obviously these people were willing to pay more than twice what the property was worth just to satisfy their racial prejudices. Borders told Senator Johnson to send back word that he would listen to a valid and clearly stated offer, and to advise that a final decision would not be reached immediately, since this property was in the name of the church and authorization to sell would require action of the official church board.

In a few days the bank president called at the church. He said he was acting on behalf of persons who did not wish to reveal their identities. He left a $3,500 check as earnest and an unsigned contract.

For nearly six weeks the banker telephoned each Monday to inquire if a decision had been reached about the farm.

During this time the barn on the farm was destroyed by fire. A white neighbor had been using the barn and some cattle were lost in the fire. There was no investigation, although one was requested by the church.

The banker was patient, and one day Borders told him that the church was ready to sell. The matter had been thoroughly discussed in the Board of Deacons. The consensus was to get out.

Reluctantly Borders agreed, although he was not then, nor is he now, ready to accept his only failure.

"I made it clear to the members of the church that I was not backing off my original idea," he said. "However, here was an opportunity for the church to double its money in three years and I considered that good stewardship. Eventually, at some future date, when the climate of rural Georgia has become more civilized toward Negro ownership of property and operation of youth camps, I intend to try again."

In early 1961 the farm was sold, the 287 acres bringing a price of $82,600 after deducting legal expenses. Subtracting the $8,000 fire-insurance money and the $2,500 realized from the pulpwood sale, from the original $45,000 purchase price, the church had realized a profit just shy of $50,000.

With the money realized from this sale, the church finished paying for the two brick apartment houses to the west of the church which had been purchased several years before. Since that purchase the church has steadily bought property in its vicinity.

Altogether about three hundred feet of property was purchased to the east along Auburn Avenue, between the Wheat Street Baptist Church and the Ebenezer Baptist Church, pastored by the Martin Luther Kings, father and son. All this property, facing Auburn Avenue and extending in depth to more than two hundred feet, has been cleared of buildings.

Another of the preacher's plans is taking shape.

"I want us to build a supermarket on that property," Borders explained. "It's got to be the very finest. No ham fat. Brilliantly lighted. The very best. You know, meat prices are high and I had hoped we would raise our own beef on the farm. I'd talked to the Swift Packing Company about dressing our beef for us . . . but maybe there'll be another farm by the time we get the supermarket completed.

"The supermarket idea came from a number of causes. One was the fact that every time we boycott a chain grocery store, trying to get a fairer percentage of jobs for Negroes, and an opportunity for Negroes to come up through the ranks to the manager's job, all we did was drive business to another chain store. Obviously we can't boycott all the food stores, so it seemed the best thing to do was to have our own supermarket."

Besides the supermarket, the pastor has plans for a beauty shop, barbershop, laundromat, and shower room. "If we're going to teach people to wear clean clothes, to get haircuts, to be neat appearing, if they expect to hold down jobs, we'll also have to scrub some of them right down to the skin," he observed in his direct practical approach to problems. "You can't just starch a man's exterior, you got to wash him clean through and through."

Other projects which came into being faster than the supermarket have delayed its construction, but it remains dear to the pastor's heart.

"Our people need to be taught business. They need to know how to run a business. If they own a business, they'll have to take additional pride in that business. Moreover, the profits can be used for their own social redemption.

"We are a poor people. In this country we started out on our own a few hundred years behind the white people. Then we suffered a hundred years of discrimination. The Metropolitan Life Insurance Company is richer, has more money, than all of the Negro businessmen in America, although we represent over a tenth of the total population. Here in Georgia the Negro represents forty percent of the population, but owns only three percent of the state's wealth.

"I advocate with all my heart the entrance of the Negro church, if that is what it takes, into the business community. We must direct some of our people's money through black channels; we must learn to be managers of our own businesses. We must place pride upon our accomplishments and upon our economic security.

"It is wonderful and remarkable for Negroes to have social opportunities and civil rights. But if they are not able to pay their bills, to the same extent they will not be able to take advantage even of some of the civil rights which we have so recently won.

"In my judgment, education, economic opportunity, the vote are of equal importance. These gains must be harmonized with religion, with the love of man for his fellow man, and his obedience to the will of God."

Often Borders is asked if he believes that a church can conduct a business and remain Christian in character.

He points out that many white denominations in their earlier days favored church businesses, patronized by church members. Likewise, he points out that Jesus spoke highly of man's need to understand money. "The two aspects are compatible, church and business, as long as we keep in mind that Jesus said man cannot live by bread alone. And remember, we already have some business at Wheat Street Baptist Church, our credit union, for instance."

After a moment's reflection, Borders added: "There is one conflict, however, on the question of the supermarket. That's the matter of Sunday openings. We have people driving to Wheat Street Church from all over Atlanta, even from outside Atlanta proper. Should these people be denied the opportunity to patronize our store—their store? I don't know. I know my daddy would horsewhip me if he was here. I've got a lot of praying to do. But we aren't going to build right now, so there's time. There's still a few parcels of land we must get. We'll want lots and lots of parking space."

9

Progress

IN THE LATE 1950's the great Interstate Highway program, largely financed by the federal government, was well under way. Across the country rights-of-way were being purchased, earth was being moved, jobs were being provided, money was being placed in circulation, and the mobile American public was about to achieve its dream of safer, high-speed interstate highways. Hardly a dissenting voice was to be heard, but not everyone had had the opportunity to speak on the highway program.

Atlanta, which badly needed modern highways, had two great interstate routes that traversed the city from north to south and from east to west. More than fifty acres of urban property were needed for the giant interchange where the two routes crossed just south of the city's central business district. Many more acres of urban property were needed for the highways themselves and for access roads.

The drafters of the interstate highway legislation had provided funds, procedures, and citizen safeguards to guarantee fair and equitable reimbursement for the property owners affected by the new highways. Through private settlements and court condemnation procedures, the highway rights-of-way through Atlanta were procured. All along, a few had asked questions, but it was not until the demolition of those dwellings standing in the path of progress began that the problem was fully recognized in terms of human lives.

The great interchange lay just south of the Wheat Street Baptist Church, and both highways traversed a part of Atlanta's inner-city Negro slum. Once clearance of the highway rights-of-way started, the truth became apparent. In this Negro slum area almost 95 percent of the property owners were absentee landlords. Nearly five thousand renter families, the pathetic little people who are termed the disadvantaged by the sociologist, were being uprooted, made homeless. These people had had no voice in the proceedings; they were truly the disfranchised citizens of a great country. Furthermore, it was discovered that there were no provisions in the highway legislation for the relocation of tenant families such as these, nor by rule and regulation could it then be proved that these unfortunates were the problem of any specific agency or department of government. (Various branches of the Federal Housing Administration could become involved in resettlement only when the problem arose because of slum clearance for urban renewal.)

The Reverend William Holmes Borders recalls: "During the time of this uprooting, these homeless people came to Wheat Street Church with their hearts in their hands, begging for advice, asking what to do. I called on the city, on the Atlanta Urban League, and the welfare department, and I literally worked around the clock myself. The problem was without adequate solution. There simply was nothing like the number of houses needed for these people who had no money, no credit, no resources, and were Negro. And the people themselves were without hope."

From the pulpit of the Wheat Street Baptist Church, and in his weekly radio broadcasts, Borders begged for housing. During these problem days, he formed the highest personal regard for Robert Thompson, the capable, understanding, and tireless executive secretary of the Atlanta Urban League, and for others who tried so earnestly to meet the problem. However, willingness to help was not enough.

Borders says: "Today I have contact with a few of these families, but for the most part they just disappeared, dropped completely out of sight, and I have never seen them since. No one really knows where they went, what suffering they endured, or even if they survived as families. The highways were a good thing. They were needed. But they were not good enough to stomp the life out of these underprivileged people who did not have the power to fight back, who did not have the know-how to provide for themselves."

The negative aftermath of this initial experience with big government programs, at least negative in terms of concern shown for the individual lives of the disadvantaged, was still fresh in mind when Borders first heard about slum clearance projects proposed by the new Atlanta Housing Authority.

"My first knowledge of the Atlanta Housing Authority," he said, "came through the local newspapers, the Atlanta *Journal*, the *Constitution*, and the Atlanta *Daily World*. I read everything which was written in these papers about the Atlanta Housing Authority, its power, its intent, and its backing and support by the city administration. I talked to friends at City Hall about the Atlanta Housing Authority. I was shown papers outlining certain broad preliminary plans then being discussed."

One day Borders concluded that his investigative research was done. He hastened to his church study and there prayed. He prayed for guidance and the wisdom to understand this leviathan of government, with its multiple interlocking bureaus, regulations and rulings, which so often appeared contradictory and always remained impersonal. It was a confusing new world. Its bureaucratic nature aroused his suspicions, and caused him to feel that little good could come to the Negro people through this channel. He had observed that such agencies had a tendency to perpetuate themselves rather than devote their best efforts to the elimination of the poverty conditions which had caused their creation. Yet in his conscience there spoke a small voice, warning that no promise of hope for the betterment of his people should be disregarded because he applied subjective reasoning rather than searching out the truth.

A lifetime in the slums, in the Lord's service, makes a realist of his handyman. Borders was indeed a realist, but an optimistic realist. He carefuly studied the purposes of the Atlanta Housing Authority, and the resources at its disposal to achieve those purposes. He knew that there were slums in every major city in America. In some of these cities slum clearance projects were already under way, new housing having replaced the blighted slum dwellings. Reason told him that slum clearance was the only hopeful answer to the urban city's blighted areas. Reason also told him there was no doubt that slum clearance would come to Atlanta.

In his beloved city of Atlanta he knew intimately the blighted areas, the slums where life was an existence, not an adventure. He firmly believed that the people living in these areas did not live there by choice. Somehow, some way, conditions over which they had no control had so completely dominated their lives that they were not able to improve their lot. Yet there was opportunity through housing for the redemption of these human lives.

The first step of the Atlanta Housing Authority, he realized, would be to procure the land. Then would follow the painful necessity of uprooting and resettling those displaced persons. As he then saw it, his task was to reduce to a minimum the pain and suffering of these unfortunate people, while trying to convince them that, despite their own suffering, slum clearance was a forward and progressive step which no one could stop.

However, Borders himself was faced with uncertainty. The federal law stated that these people being uprooted must be fairly treated and adequately housed. But he had observed through his years in the ministry that there had been many instances of other laws which had been disregarded when Negro rights were involved. What if he told his people they would be adequately and fairly cared for, and they were not? Would the administration of this law be different? How much had wishful thinking influenced his decision to support slum clearance?

The answer to his problem, he decided, lay with the people who were to administer the Atlanta Housing Authority. If they administered slum clearance fairly and with a sense of kindness, according to the federal law, and the people could return to the new housing, then this would be a good thing. However, if slum clearance was not administered according to federal law, the situation would be bad, perhaps even worse than at present. He determined to learn all he could about the Atlanta Housing Authority and the people in charge.

Previously, as he worked for the betterment of the Negro people in Atlanta, he had established personal contact with the mayor, aldermen, and city officials. He believed in keeping open direct lines of communication, especially across racial lines. With this in mind, he volunteered for every task and committee involved with slum clearance of which he could learn. In this way he was able to observe the people in charge of the Atlanta Housing Authority. In Borders' own words, he found these people, "scientific, technical, skilled. In many instances, they were kind. But they had a job to do. The very nature of that job appeared to some people to be cruel."

One committee of which he was a member was headed by L. D. Milton, president of the Citizens Trust Company. This committee's specific task was to reach directly those persons who would become personally involved through the initial land procurement phase of the housing program. The task of this committee was neither easy nor rewarding. An emancipated people, suffering from a century of disfranchisement, were filled with fear and distrust. The highway incident was fresh in their minds.

In these meetings Borders found himself telling an often hostile audience that the housing authority was like a surgeon. The surgeon means the patient all the good in the world, but because of the nature of the disease, he must use a knife. It was difficult to convince these people that slum clearance surgery was necessary, or that those in charge of the housing authority were kind.

Often it seemed the sole accomplishment of these meetings was to convince the people present that Borders favored their immediate evacuation because he was working hand in glove with the Atlanta Housing Authority.

He saw his own image becoming tarnished, and he fretted over this. He saw his own people blocking progress of needed housing projects designed to help them, and he fretted over possible reactions because of their intransigence.

His wife feared for his health and begged him to withdraw from his slum clearance activities. Politely, as was his nature, he explained that he could not do so, in conscience to his pledge to God to preach the gospel and to be his brother's keeper.

She had expected this very answer.

At a community meeting on the west side of Atlanta, attended by M. B. Saterfield, executive director of the Atlanta Housing Authority, Borders publicly asked if it would be possible for an individual or an institutional organization to sponsor a housing project on land the Altanta Housing Authority had obtained and cleared.

Borders had made it a practice to challenge, probe, and irritate the authority's leadership as he sought to resolve his own gnawing doubts over his support of slum clearance. He waited now for Saterfield's reply. Without hesitation he answered, "Yes."

Thinking back on that evening, Borders says: "Honestly, I did not believe him. I did not believe he understood that I meant a Negro individual or organization. If he had understood me, I felt he surely would have talked more about character investigation, financial solvency, and cash reserves. I did not believe him, but I intended to find out. I did so by telephoning Washington, D.C., where I spoke to several persons in the Federal Housing Administration. I was told that there were federal programs which would sponsor fifty percent of the financing, ninety percent of the financing, and even one hundred percent of the financing in the case of nonprofit organizations, if such an organization was of long standing and good character and would warrant that sort of trust. Furthermore, that the racial complexion of the sponsoring institution was of no concern and had no bearing upon decisions relative to a housing loan under the FHA.

"I sat in my study a long time after hanging up the telephone. I had been telling these people, my people, my friends, that the housing authority would take the land and that there was nothing they could do about it. Also, I had assured them that the housing authority would treat them fairly, would secure them housing, and offer them first choice of the new housing once it was available. Now, suddenly, here I was in my own mind entertaining thoughts that I wanted this land, that I wanted the Wheat Street Baptist Church to sponsor the housing project. Would these people understand? If they found I was personally involved, would they continue to believe me? Could I truly handle a project of this size?

"The only problem with great dreams, with reaching for the heights, is that your problems have to soar with you. I did a lot of praying that afternoon."

Just across Auburn Avenue, a block distant from the church, was an area crowded with crumbling slum dwellings. The pastor knew that the Atlanta Housing Authority had made a preliminary survey of 22½ acres of this land with slum clearance and urban renewal in mind.

He left the church and walked over to this tract of land.

"I walked around that property more often than Joshua around the walls of Jericho. It was dark when I returned to the church and I knew that I must be mad. I got down on my knees and prayed to God.

"Way down in the bottom of my heart, I still couldn't believe that this valuable land, within eight walking minutes from Five Points in the heart of Atlanta's business district, would ever be permitted to fall into the hands of Negroes. It was 22½ acres of the finest property in Georgia. I simply didn't believe it possible to secure this land for Negroes, but I vowed I would try.

"Even to try seemed farfetched, outrageous, so I decided not to tell anyone of my plan. This is one of the few times that I did not confide in my wife. I was afraid that she might hear me out but say nothing. Then, several days later, she would say, 'Now Holmes, about that housing project...' If I didn't dare tell my wife, I reasoned I certainly could not tell the church, not even my wonderful and loyal Board of Deacons. This was one of those dreams by which man soars, by which he achieves something beyond his known abilities, beyond even the dreams he has previously dreamed. I had to ascertain if I could pilot myself in the stratosphere of my new hopes, where I wanted to lead my church. I had to prove my success before I dared mention my intentions to anyone."

In the days that followed, as it became more and more evident that the Atlanta Housing Authority was going to procure title to this 22½ acres, Borders walked through, around, literally all over the land.

"I was closely associated with the occupants of that land by day and sometimes by night. They asked all kinds of questions: 'Are they taking our homes?' 'When must we leave?' 'Will we be allowed to return?' 'How long will we have?' 'Negroes suffer everything.' 'I have been living here all my life.' 'It's not what it ought to be, but it's home to me.' 'I was born in this house; even though it is a shack I love it.' 'I want to remain.' 'I do not want to be disturbed.' 'Negroes have such a hard time.' 'We are always being disturbed.' 'We have absolutely no freedom when they can take away our houses.'"

Speaking now from his heart, with assurance that the law was meant to be interpreted alike for all men, regardless of race, he answered these frightened, unhappy people. "This place is sweet to you, and I understand. We're going to make it sweeter. You will be able to return to this very spot, almost. You will have first choice after construction is completed."

Some did not believe. Others took the pastor seriously. Day by day he repeated these words, these promises, over and over.

One day his wife said, "Holmes, do you really think you can do it? The housing project, I mean?"

"I'm convinced they'll let me try," he answered her. "I'll give it my very best effort."

"I know you will," she replied. "The children and I have been praying that you will succeed. Oh, Holmes, do you realize what this will mean? Not in terms of apartments or houses, but in evidence, evidence in Atlanta, in Georgia, in America, that the Negro wants to and has the ability to assume his share of responsibility. The time will come, Holmes, when the term disadvantaged will not be synonymous with the word Negro."

The Atlanta Housing Authority did buy this tract of land, although in some instances it had to go to court to complete the purchase. This, despite the fact that the houses were dilapidated, windows out, fences sagging, no paint, and leaking roofs. Few of the occupants owned these homes. As tenants they paid excessive rentals, higher than in other parts of the city for comparable space.

As these people established broader contacts with agencies and people working toward the goal of slum clearance, the realization slowly formed that they had been exploited, gouged. This left wounds that could not be healed by the mere promise of better housing.

The housing authority had to move according to law, which was often a slow process, and especially so through the courts. Yet Borders feels it was important for these people to see the power of the law at work through the courts. The people saw appraisers evaluate the worth of the property, and in some instances go to court to uphold that valuation and bring condemnation proceedings against the absentee landlords.

Agencies were established to assist the dispossessed tenants find new housing, but the pastor shouldered more than his share of the burden and worked long and hard hours to help these people. After the highway uprooting, people had been permanently lost to the church and to the community. The housing project, he vowed, would be different. It was.

In many instances Borders went with the people to check houses offered for rent or sale in a new neighborhood. Many of these were in the Whiteford section of Atlanta. In the few instances where houses were purchased, he helped negotiate terms between seller and buyer, assisting in the determination of how much money could be paid down and if the buyer's income would permit him to carry the monthly payments.

More often he engaged a truck and did manual labor, loading the family's possessions on the truck. In Atlanta there is a law which prohibits moving at night. When the head of the household had to work until five or six o'clock and was unable to take a day off, it was essential that the truck be loaded and ready to roll when the head of the family reached home. Borders drove his car ahead, followed by the truck. Some of the family would be in the preacher's car, some in the truck.

"There were heartrending experiences with these relocations of families," Borders recalls. "At the last minute, most people were reluctant to leave. They were afraid. They did not know how they would be accepted in the new community. They resented being forced to make adjustments without choice. Although many families improved themselves by moving into better housing, the fact that they had had to move disturbed them. It emphasized all over again their personal insecurity, their hand-to-mouth existence."

The process of evacuating the area strung out over several months. There were some touching scenes as little children rode the city bus from their new community back to their old slum community to play with friends who still remained in the old neighborhood.

This time the church did not lose track of its membership. The children who had moved from the neighborhood were brought back to Sunday school by the church buses used during the week to bring children to the nursery school. The Wheat Street Baptist Church buses still travel to the far corners of the city each Sunday morning.

A few families joined churches in their new communities, but most returned to Wheat Street Baptist Church for the Sunday morning worship service. As Borders says, "We are still a fellowship and we are still very happy together."

Nearly two years elapsed from the initial land purchase to the time the last house had been demolished and the property was made available for purchase.

The Atlanta Housing Authority had divided the property into fourteen plots. They willingly gave information on the property to Borders, or to anyone else who expressed an interest in it, whether these persons were concerned with the people or with profits. At this point the law was quite specific. All persons could bid for the property.

After learning all he could about the property, Borders called on Earl H. Metzger, director of urban renewal for the Atlanta Housing Authority, and told him he wanted to bid on the land.

"Which of the fourteen plots do you wish to bid on, Reverend Borders?" he asked.

"I want to bid on all fourteen plots, or on none," the preacher replied.

Metzger looked up in surprise. "You're Reverend William Holmes Borders of the Wheat Street Baptist Church, aren't you? Well, Reverend, you are talking about three hundred and fifty thousand dollars, and unless you have that much money, or unless some institution or organization supporting you can lend you that much money immediately, your bid would be meaningless."

Borders thanked him and left. He had taken Metzger very seriously; he believed he knew what he was talking about. His immediate task was to prove that he did have that sort of financial backing.

Borders called on his friend, E. M. Martin, secretary of the Atlanta Life Insurance Company. Before the turn of the century, the Atlanta Life Insurance Company had started as a burial insurance fund in the Wheat Street Baptist Church. Now it was a $60-million life insurance company. The church had borrowed $200,000 from the Atlanta Life to finance the Christian Education Building and had repaid the money in five, rather than twelve, years. The church's reputation was good, so the pastor did not hesitate to tell Martin of his plan for the church to sponsor a housing project, the first of its kind in the nation. He explained that he needed immediate confirmation of the availability of half a million dollars to guarantee the land purchase.

Martin led the way into the office of the late Norris B. Herndon, president of the Atlanta Life Insurance Company. A few minutes later they returned to Martin's office, where he dictated a letter stating that the Wheat Street Baptist Church could draw up to half a million dollars upon call of the pastor.

Borders asked to wait until Martin's secretary finished typing the letter. He wanted to deliver this vital document personally to Metzger. As he sat waiting, listening to the secretary's fingers fly lightly across the keyboard, he couldn't help but feel a touch of personal pride and love for his city. He had preached in Atlanta for over twenty years and hadn't earned half a million dollars, but after twenty years as a preacher he could borrow that sum of money.

The letter was delivered to Metzger, duly noted, and Borders was advised how and when to file his sealed bid for the property.

There was a strong desire on the part of many influential persons, Negro and white, to see this property rehabilitated and put back into housing. It was a federal requirement that housing would go back, but not necessarily through Negro sponsorship. The pastor sensed, from the reception of his plan at the Atlanta Life Insurance Company, that the Negro business community would support him in this endeavor. He would seek their active support later.

Now he had to see about the white community's support.

His first call was the mayor's office. He did not believe in taking independent action, which might reach the mayor's attention without having first stated his plans to that official. Mayor Hartsfield listened attentively. "Who would oppose you, Preacher? If you want to take that much responsibility, you should be supported. I'll support you."

This was not the type of project that the mayor or other white businessmen wished to support publicly at that time. The church might not submit the best bid, which would place political backers in a poor light with the party having the highest bid. Also, this was a nonprofit venture, which of itself is not always understood or appreciated by some of the business community. However, one after another of the white leaders of Atlanta pledged Borders their personal support.

This, in a quiet and unobtrusive way, they gave. Men spoke to other men. All agreed it would be a good project for Atlanta on the basis of interracial goodwill. Since nothing else like this had happened anywhere in the United States, they were proud that it should happen first in Atlanta. The preacher from the Wheat Street Baptist Church was assured that his housing project was quietly discussed at luncheon or dinner tables at the Chamber of Commerce, at civic club meetings, and in private conferences.

"You have our support, Preacher," the mayor told him.

He now talked of his project with L. D. Milton, president of the Citizens Trust Company, who had headed the first committee on slum clearance on which he had participated publicly. This influential Negro business leader promised to enlist the support of the Negro business community. Martin also advised the pastor to see Robert A. Thompson of the Atlanta Urban League. The project had already reached such proportions that Borders needed expert help, and this, Thompson provided.

Thompson soon had letters endorsing the project from seventy fraternal, labor, and civic organizations in the Negro business community.

He also found out that the best-informed attorney in Atlanta on matters of federal housing legislation was Lewis Cenker. Thompson and Borders called on Cenker, a man of the Jewish faith. Their request was a bit unusual. They were interested in Section 221 D-3 of the Federal Housing Authority regulations, subtitle: Nonprofit Sponsorship. As they understood the law, the United States government offered 100 percent replacement loans, including cost of land, construction, architectural fees, legal and organizational fees, and interest on moneys borrowed, available on forty-year loans at 3 percent interest.

They had never attempted to put together such a program, nor did they know of anyone in the United States who had. Cenker had been recommended as one who knew his way through the maze of Federal Housing Authority regulations. Would he become their adviser and attorney, with the understanding that any fee was contingent upon the Wheat Street

Baptist Church's not only procuring the land but also obtaining a government loan for the housing?

Cenker agreed to their proposal. Its challenge interested him, and he believed it was for the good of Atlanta.

They next approached James Wise of the Atlanta architectural firm of Wise, Simpson, and Aiken, one of the largest in the country. Wise also felt challenged and agreed to provide the necessary architectural plans on a strictly contingent basis.

Wise made an architectural sketch of the garden-type apartments he envisioned for the property. Borders and Thompson were delighted. In short order they had submitted to the Atlanta Housing Authority copies of the proposed housing project as evidence of their intended use of the land. Copies of these drawings were reproduced and shown to certain interested individuals who had pledged their support. They then asked bankers and real estate people not to bid on the property, taking the lead here from the course being followed by their white friends.

On the day that bidding was closed, not one single bid for the property was submitted from within the state of Georgia, other than that of the Wheat Street Baptist Church. However, there were out-of-state bids.

The sealed bids were to be opened at City Hall. Borders recalls the event: "Our interracial, interfaith team of Bob Thompson, Negro-Protestant; Lewis Cenker, White-Jewish; Jim Wise, White-Protestant; and myself, Negro-Protestant; were almost too excited to talk. I don't think Bob Thompson had slept for several nights. Among ourselves we had debated the amount of our bid up to the last minute, and now I believe each of us wishes we had raised our final figure."

A city alderman opened the sealed bids. A firm from New Orleans bid $424,000, but that was the second highest bidder.

The Wheat Street Baptist Church was the successful bidder for the land, with a submitted bid of $450,000.

This strange and optimistic quartet of men, all southerners by birth or adoption, who were talking not about racial issues but about problem solutions, were now ready to pool their talents for the benefit of the disadvantaged, under the sponsorship of a Negro church, pastored by a man whose father had been a slave.

10

Teamwork

UNTIL THE OPENING of the sealed bids for the purchase of the slum clearance property, no one in the church knew of the Wheat Street Baptist Church's involvement or had the slightest inkling of their pastor's plan. The Reverend William Holmes Borders knew that the newspapers would pick up the information of the church's successful bid and that it would be known throughout Atlanta the next day.

He lost no time and called a special meeting of the Board of Deacons for that very night.

Formerly the church had had a business meeting once a month. However, after the publication of the detailed monthly record of financial receipts and disbursements, an act which once had rocked the church's very foundation, attendance at the monthly business meetings dwindled. Therefore, power to deal with major financial matters of the church was vested in the Board of Deacons, and the business meeting became an annual affair. It was now an absolute necessity for the pastor to have a positive vote by the board.

"Indeed," says Borders as he recalls that moment, "no pastor has a right to go so far with such gigantic tasks unless he has had the vote of the church. I think this is generally true, although I felt it was not true in this case. For the initial phase of my work on our housing project I proceeded on faith, faith in God and faith in the love and confidence of my people as their preacher.

"I made this questionable decision for this reason: I knew that if my dreams, my plans, which I still could hardly convince myself might happen to Negroes, were revealed to the Board of Deacons and to the church, there would be tremendous discussion and doubt. Many persons would not believe that our church would ever be permitted to purchase this land, or that the federal government would lend us that much money. They were not as close to the facts of the situation as I was, and could hardly be expected to overcome quickly these same basic doubts which had plagued me for months. In the long run, I believe the church would have voted its confidence in me then if I had gone to them first, but I felt I lacked the time and the strength for such discussion. Ahead of me there lay so much to do, to accomplish. So I chose my unusual method to cut off unnecessary and wasteful discussion. If the doubters were right, no damage would be done through my efforts. If I was right, every spirit in our church would be uplifted and cheered. Therefore I went ahead with my plans."

The Board of Deacons heard their preacher through with little comment. When Borders sat down, the chairman of the board looked at the smiling faces and, with hardly a word of discussion, called for a vote. The Wheat Street Baptist Church was unanimously placed in the business of developing a housing project.

The word was out. That Sunday the Wheat Street Baptist

Church was overflowing. Part of the crowd had to be accommodated in the auditorium of the Christian Education Building. Again Borders told what he had done in the church's name, and asked the members for their vote of confidence. The vote was unanimous, but that did not mean that everyone believed the plan would work.

W. J. Weams, chairman of the Board of Deacons, described the situation this way: "Most people were so happy they could hardly contain themselves. There were others who wanted to believe, who tried hard to believe, but just couldn't make the grade in so short a time. There were also a few who were afraid that we had bitten off more than we could chew and would be disgraced and our people set back because of our failure."

"After the vote we sang a few of the great hymns of the church," recalls the pastor. "Hymns like 'Lift Him Up, Christ Is All,' and 'How Great Thou Art.' Then, after a prayer of thanksgiving to a merciful and almighty God, we went over to the Christian Education Building and had dinner together and talked about the future, our future. The members of the Board of Deacons circulated through the crowds, penetrating one discussion group after another. Mr. Weams, here, did a tremendous job.

"Let me tell you about Mr. Weams," the pastor adds. "He has had one employer for more than forty years. He was one of seven children, five sons and two daughters. His mother raised the family, and today all five sons are either deacons or preachers. When I asked her how this happened, his mother told me, 'I kept them boys in the field, in the school, and in the church.' It is men like Mr. Weams, and women too, who have made Wheat Street Church."

While the church was getting accustomed to its new image, more than one white businessman telephoned to tell the pastor: "Preacher, I had serious doubts that you and your associates, church and civic groups, would be able to get the financial backing and organization necessary for this project. That you have done so is remarkable."

In one manner or another, each then proceeded to point out the marvelous and positive example this housing project would present to all detractors of the Negro people. Here were the most disadvantaged people of a metropolitan city wanting to assume responsibility of a financial and leadership role in developing a multimillion-dollar housing project sorely needed by the community.

As each man finished his promises of vigorous and positive support, the preacher intoned a quiet "Amen." "Yes, Lord," he murmured, "you've brought us a long way, a long, long way."

While Borders was busy informing the Wheat Street Baptist Church of its involvement in what was to be called the Wheat Street Garden Homes, Thompson was busy implementing a sizable check list.

The priority items on his agenda were:

(1) The first step, to engage a first-rate and knowledgeable lawyer of FHA rules and regulations on a contingency basis had been accomplished with Lewis Cenker's acceptance of the job.

(2) The second step was also accomplished with the similar employment of the Atlanta architectural firm of Wise, Simpson, and Aiken.

When Thompson asked James Wise if it would be possible for his firm to employ a Negro, it took but a minute for him to answer. "Well, yes," he replied, "we employ a Japanese, a German, an Englishman, and white Americans. Why not a Negro American too?"

Shortly Raiford Newman, a graduate of Howard University, was hired as consulting architect for the Wheat Street Garden Homes, on the staff of Wise, Simpson, and Aiken.

(3) The third point was to apprise the Federal Housing Administration (FHA) of the preliminary proposal, and to request on-site appraisal of the land and adjacent surroundings by that agency, as well as to secure their advice at this early stage of planning.

Thompson, with the church providing his expense money, prepared for the first of several visits to Washington to see FHA officials.

(4) The next point was to confer with officials of the Federal National Mortgage Association (FNMA) relative to taking the permanent mortgage. This too had to be accomplished in part in Washington.

(5) Next on the agenda was to maintain negotiations with the Atlanta Life Insurance Company on a direct basis by keeping their officials informed of each action taken. Also to keep close relations with the officers of the Citizens Trust Company, who were to serve as agents for the Atlanta Life Insurance Company.

(6) Finding a local bank willing to make the construction loan was the next point on Thompson's check list.

J. O. Childs and Myer Holtz of the Trust Company of Georgia, Atlanta's third largest bank, were approached. The problems of getting a five-million-dollar construction loan with minimum service charges for a nonprofit corporation took some explaining. Thompson and Borders carefully went through each step of the program, the sponsors, the church, the Atlanta Urban League, the permanent mortgage, and negotiations in Washington. The bankers remarked that all the major banks in Atlanta would be invited to participate in a loan of this size and nature. Since then, bankers have learned much more about Section 221 D-3 of the FHA regulations, even on the nonprofit sponsorship section, and gladly make construction loans under provisions of this title.

(7) The last important item on Thompson's list was to keep in touch with the civic, political, business, fraternal, and trade-union organizations that had endorsed the housing project by letter. Their continued support was needed as evidence the community wanted the Wheat Street Garden Homes.

Attorney Cenker was also busy. Besides drafting the necessary papers for the FHA office, he was busy with:

(1) Forming a subsidiary corporation, Church Homes, Inc., which would manage the Wheat Street Garden Homes through a board of directors.

Twenty members of the Wheat Street Baptist Church were chosen to serve as directors, with J. D. Blayton, Sr., president of the Atlanta Urban League and president of the Mutual Federal Savings and Loan Association, the only non-Wheat Street member of the board. (He provided invaluable service in setting up the books and accounting procedures.)

(2) Obtaining and appointing an attorney for the new Church Homes, Inc., corporation. This was to be A. T. Walden, a lifelong member of the Wheat Street Baptist Church, and a community leader.

(3) Securing a charter for the new corporation from the state of Georgia.

(4) Raising the necessary funds from the Atlanta Life Insurance Company and having them properly transferred to the Atlanta Housing Authority in exchange for land titles.

(5) Arranging for the FHA housing loan and mortgage. Although attorney, architect, Urban League secretary, and pastor were all specialists in their own areas, they worked together harmoniously on all phases of the work. This was essential, for despite the cooperation of governmental agencies, these agencies did require a tremendous amount of paper work

covering all areas of the project. One evening as Attorney Cenker was listing various funds under numerous headings on a large sheet of legal forms, all bearing government imprints, he turned to Borders and asked for his opinion. Borders shook his head. "Mr. Cenker, you go right ahead and put those figures down in their proper columns, and I'll pray that you get them in the proper place."

Just as soon as the architects had preliminary plans roughed out, and the attorney had all his financial figures in the right columns, and Thompson and Borders had their progress reports up to date, they were called to Washington to meet with Robert Weaver, then head of the FHA.

Borders describes that meeting. "We were greeted very cordially by Weaver, who convinced us within thirty seconds that he really knew all about our proposed project. Bob Thompson described the land as he unrolled blueprints of the plot. I next told him of the sponsoring institution, the Wheat Street Baptist Church, which he already knew about by reputation. I described the community. I told him of the slum area, and of the people who had moved out, and of our plans to bring back as many of those people as wanted to come. I told him that we had secured the services of the finest architectural firm in Atlanta and introduced him to Mr. James Wise, who discussed the architectural plans. Mr. Weaver already knew Attorney Lewis Cenker, who went over the financial proposal.

"When we had finished, Mr. Weaver said that our proposal fitted into the law better than anything that he had seen since becoming Federal Housing Administrator. He assured us that our project would have the support of his office, of their regional offices, as well as members of their Atlanta office. While we were still present, he dictated a letter to this effect."

Borders met Weaver on other occasions, although these

were not strictly business meetings. On each occasion inquiry was made about the housing project, promises of his continued support were given, and Weaver insisted that he be called personally if he could be of assistance.

Thompson, in his reports to the FHA and in a speech given to a national assembly of Urban League representatives, stressed the uniqueness of this operating team, this interracial, interfaith body of men. "Our personal contacts were tremendous. Between us, there was not an office in Atlanta which we could not enter and find someone we knew seated across the desk. Our diverse backgrounds and cultures, coupled with an obvious dedication to the task, was impressive.

"However, let me point out that this project could not have been accomplished if it had not been for the leadership of the Reverend William Holmes Borders. This leadership ability was first exemplified in his program for the Wheat Street Baptist Church. Here he built up both the membership and the facilities, meaning the magnificent church structure and the Christian Education Building. Remember, he had borrowed several hundred thousand dollars for these programs and always repaid the church loans ahead of time. The Reverend Borders' willingness to put his entire church program and resources back of the Wheat Street Garden Homes had a great bearing upon the success of that project.

"Also, when the FHA investigators started checking on the solvency and character of the Wheat Street Baptist Church, the Reverend Borders brought out a quarter of a century's records showing monthly cash intake and outgo. It showed that on some Sundays the collection at Wheat Street Baptist Church exceeds three thousand dollars, that the average Sunday collection is well above two thousand dollars, and that expenses have always been regulated and balanced to income.

"After going over those records, I do not recall that the

investigation of the character and solvency of the Wheat Street Baptist Church continued any further."

Once again, a decision which at one time had threatened the position of the pastor, now supported him in his time of need. The FHA loan was approved.

The following editorial from the December 6, 1961, issue of the Atlanta *Daily World* is typical of the community reaction.

A Worthy and Needed Project

The City of Atlanta is a step nearer in solving the problem of urban redevelopment because of the effort of Church Homes, Inc., and its purchase of a 22 acre tract of land in the northeast section of the city for the building of a multi-million dollar housing project. Church Homes, Inc., its 20 member Board of Directors, and the Atlanta Urban League, are to be congratulated in announcing their plans for 520 units of housing to aid the acute dwelling problem in this city.

Reverend William Holmes Borders, spokesman for the sponsoring organization, pastor of the Wheat Street Baptist Church, is to be commended in having his church lead the way in this development.

Urban development and expressway projects have displaced many Negroes near the city center and have forced them outward in the search for living space.

Church Homes, Inc., as a non-profit organization, has worked out a fine solution to help alleviate the area's housing problems. They have further rendered a document for direction to future development within the framework of the City of Atlanta and other areas of America.

Negro population within the city is increasing more rapidly than is the white. It had risen 106 per cent in the three decades since 1930. The number of white residents, in comparison, has increased by a total of 67 per cent during the same period of time. This growth has placed extreme pressure on the older Negro areas near the city center, and has contributed to slum congestion. The plan presented by this group is one way of handling the Negro community today and deserves the praises of all Atlantans.

At this time, after some twenty years as mayor of Atlanta, William B. Hartsfield announced that he was stepping down from office.

Borders knew that he and his people were losing a friend. It had not always been so. There had been a segregationist tone to the mayor's original refusal to consider Negro policemen. In the mind of Borders, Mayor Hartsfield had grown in office, through experience he had learned to administer to the needs of all people in Atlanta.

Borders says: "I hope I am safe in saying that William B. Hartsfield learned as much from some of the Negroes as he did from any other group of citizens in Atlanta. We sat with him in his office, in other appointed places, and talked to him frankly about problems of Atlanta. Specifically we talked to him about the problems of the Negro in Atlanta. There were times when he opposed us, yet exhibited understanding. There were times when he opposed us because he thought that what we were asking could not be done. But we did get Negro policemen. We did desegregate the buses, and we did get Negro bus drivers and Negro bus employees. The Negro policemen in Atlanta have full authority under the law. And remember, this all began with Mayor Hartsfield. It began way back with Negro voter registration. I not only learned to respect Mayor Hartsfield, but I learned to love him as a man. He was not all that he should have been, but neither am I, neither is any person in the world. There has been only one perfect person, and that was Jesus."

The man chosen to follow Mayor Hartsfield was Ivan Allen, Jr., a native-born Atlantan, whose father had opened an office equipment company in Atlanta well before the turn of the century. Allen was "born, bred, buttered, and spanked in Atlanta." Financially independent, he was a Presbyterian and a Christian in the finest sense of the word.

As soon as Borders heard of Allen's interest in running for the office of mayor, he called on this Atlanta business leader in his office. "I told him that if he ran for mayor of Atlanta, he might not get his own vote, but he would get mine. Then I steered our conversation around to the Wheat Street Garden Homes. I just happened to have plans and blueprints ready to show him. He told me that anyone who opposed such a project had no heart, no understanding. That on pure principle, our project had his support. He stated he would gladly back it."

Allen was elected and Borders maintained his direct line of communication, across racial lines, to the financial and political leaders of Atlanta.

Mayor Allen's support has been tangible in many ways. For instance, it was discovered that a sewer line, nine feet in diameter, ran through the property the church had purchased. The sewer had been installed in 1890. When the FHA learned this, they advised the church that government-sponsored housing could not be constructed above the sewer for fear of cave-ins.

Since the sewer was city property, Borders took this matter directly to Mayor Allen. The mayor said he did not know what could be done, but promised that if the church would buy the materials, the city would provide the engineers and labor needed to reroute the sewer. It was his opinion that the city had a moral responsibility in the matter.

Later he telephoned Borders and told him that the city had decided to reroute the entire sewer and shoulder the estimated $65,000 cost. He had been told by city engineers that a seventy-year-old sewer had served its usefulness. Responsible persons in the city administration agreed with him that the city had a moral responsibility to see that this land, now owned by the Wheat Street Baptist Church, met FHA requirements of suitability for the proposed housing project.

"This was but one of the unseen rewards and helps," says Borders, "which came to the Wheat Street Garden Homes. It didn't just have to happen.

"Ivan Allen is a great mayor, a tribute he has earned on merit and performance in office. He has aided the entire city with our great municipal stadium and our new auditorium. But also, he has worked unceasingly for the improvement of the lot of the disadvantaged citizens in Atlanta. He has built new firehouses in the Negro community and has employed Negro firemen. He went to Washington, D.C., to testify in favor of civil rights, the only southern mayor to do so.

"It was wonderful that he was mayor of Atlanta while we built the Wheat Street Garden Homes. One day he came to my church office and picked me up in his automobile. We rode around the project and he asked what suggestions I had. We had the project engineer and his assistant with us. As a result of that tour, he promised us more brilliant street lighting, paved streets, curbs, and storm sewers. These things have been done. They should be done, but in many cities and in many instances they are not done. There was no hesitancy here. The mayor of Atlanta took the lead."

It took time for the architect to complete his plans, to secure the necessary FHA approval of them, and for the attorney to finish his work. Meanwhile the property stood idle month after month.

Slums breed a state of poverty of mind, soul, and body. The natural tendency of the slum dweller is not to build but to destroy, to be negative. The sight of that vacant property, for which there had been glowing promises of new housing but a few months before, promises which had encouraged the private luxury of hopes long denied, now commenced to generate the slum's normal negative attitude.

Within the Negro community there arose doubts and words of grumbling. Also, there were persons in the white community, although not numerous, who hoped the project would fail. This was sufficient to start rumors that the church didn't really own title to the land; that the contract had been withdrawn; that the church had bitten off more than it could chew.

This was a difficult period for the pastor, although he was close enough to the work of the project to take courage in its progress. The extent of the grumbling, however, reached the point where he had to take official notice of it in the church's Board of Deacons meeting. He explained the necessity for the architect to have sufficient time to draw plans, to write out specifications, to interest a large enough number of contractors to ensure competitive bids as required by law. Furthermore, he showed copies of papers in the possession of Cenker, their attorney, proving that the land title was now registered in the name of their subsidiary corporation, Church Homes, Inc.

With the renewed support of his Board of Deacons, the grumblings elsewhere were not so unbearable.

The time came when the architect had finished his work, and all plans and specifications had necessary FHA approval. The plans were released to as many contractors as wanted to bid. The date for the opening of the construction bids was set for four o'clock one afternoon early in April, 1963. Interested persons gathered in the auditorium of the Christian Education Building. The secretary of the church opened the sealed bids. The total cost and stated time limit of each submitted contract was read aloud. In all, ten firms submitted bids for the first half of the project, 280 apartments in three-story garden-type brick buildings.

The low bid was $2,975,000 and had a time stipulation of twelve months. This bid was lowest by $180,000. It was submitted by the Atlanta-based construction firm of Jet, Banks, and Russell, a Negro firm.

This bid was accepted.

Thompson and Borders immediately took the contractor's representative to the Trust Company of Georgia. Despite no previous experience in servicing government-guaranteed loans of this type, the bank agreed to make a construction loan to the contractor in the amount of $2,355,000, to cover construction of the first 280 apartments of the Wheat Street Garden Homes.

The contractor was required by the sponsor, Church Homes, Inc., to negotiate a 100 percent performance bond, which was done. Allegedly, at that time this was the largest such performance bond given to a Negro contractor.

Thompson also called on the Atlanta Labor Council, AFL-CIO, and secured an endorsement of the Wheat Street Garden Homes. "The Labor Council's endorsement of the project was, in my opinion, very magnanimous," says Thompson. "By terms of the contract, the contractor was not required to pay prevailing wages. It should also be remembered that at that time there were persons in the building construction trades who were unemployed in the Atlanta area. The Labor Council endorsed the project because they knew the great need for decent housing in this section of Atlanta. Their action was wonderful, and was most beneficial to all parties concerned."

Borders immediately urged the contractor to get some equipment on the property and start construction, so that the community might see tangible proof of progress. Two weeks after the bidding, the contractor moved in machinery and started work. That Sunday, April 26, 1963, ground-breaking ceremonies were held.

Two high school bands played for the more than two thousand persons who attended the ceremonies. Among those seated on the platform were Mayor Allen and members of the Atlanta Board of Aldermen; Frank Daniels, FHA Multi-Housing Division Chief, from Washington; Dr. A. L. Thompson of the Atlanta FHA office (who had been a great help and was to be of even more assistance); Congressman Charles Weltner; Georgia State Senator LeRoy Johnson; officials and representatives of the Atlanta Life Insurance Company and the Citizens Trust Company.

The mayor and the pastor each turned the traditional spadeful of earth. Many of the speakers admitted this was a tremendous undertaking for the sponsoring institution, the Wheat Street Baptist Church. They cited it as evidence that the church was willing to shoulder even more than its share of community responsibility to advance the progress of those persons who lived in its vicinity. The speakers also cited the cooperative effort of private business, of government, of church, and of individuals, which had truly made this an interracial, interfaith, intercity endeavor. With such an origin, it was but fitting that the Wheat Street Garden Homes would be open to everyone who qualified, regardless of race or faith.

Refreshments were served by the Coca-Cola Company. Long after the officials had departed, people still stood on the housing project land, or walked along the foundation excavations, picked up and felt the soil, told of the shacks that had been torn down on this site, and spoke of the promises ahead. It was a joyous, happy occasion.

That evening Borders, as was his custom, prayed to God.

For many months he had been asking the Lord to grant the church this property for the housing project. He was aware that he did not even know about many elements connected with this venture, much less understand them. He knew that he did not have the money, the influence, or the power to secure all the help needed. He readily understood that he needed not only help from above, but the support of human hands and hearts as well.

The pastor says: "I believe with all my heart that God intervened; that God intervened, I am positive, certain beyond a doubt. This church-sponsored housing project could never have happened without the guidance of the Spirit of the eternal God."

Filled with this conviction, he prayed that night with a joyous heart, in a spirit of thanksgiving.

11

Housing

UNDER THE TITLE "Another Atlanta First," the June, 1963, issue of the *Atlantan*, a publication of the Atlanta Chamber of Commerce, carried this article:

> "I don't believe it could have happened any place except in Atlanta," a prominent Negro minister declared here recently. The Reverend William H. Borders, Pastor of the Wheat Street Baptist Church had reference to the considerable cooperation, understanding and approval provided by many local white and Negro leaders whose joint efforts are yielding Atlanta the first Negro sponsored rental housing project of its kind in the nation. If he underestimates the quality of race relations in other cities, they can no doubt appreciate and forgive his enthusiasm. It is generated by the realization of his congregation's hopes and dreams and prayers and plans to develop more than 500 new downtown apartments for middle income Negro families.
>
> Construction began last month on the first 280 units, which are to be ready for occupancy by the end of the next year.

Plans call for an additional 240 units soon thereafter. All will be in three story garden type apartment buildings in the Butler Street Renewal Area, less than one mile east of Five Points, and will rent from $70.00 to $75.00 a month. The initial phase represents the first such housing development in the country to be sponsored by Negroes under Section 221 D-3 of the Federal Housing Administration's program for low cost multi-family housing.

Approximately the entire project is being built by local Negro contracting firms.

Although the contractor was Negro, the labor force was fully integrated. There were white foremen working with Negro crews for a Negro contractor, and white laborers working under a Negro foreman for a Negro contractor. There were no labor troubles. This was not the first time the building trades had been integrated in Atlanta, but at that time this represented the largest of such projects.

According to the pastor, some of that labor force stops by even yet to talk to the apartment manager or talks to the pastor at his study. However, when construction started, not all of the labor force, which reached nearly fifteen hundred men, knew the pastor by sight, or understood that the neighboring church was sponsoring the housing they were erecting.

This led to several amusing incidents, but the pastor's favorite story is of the day he was sidewalk superintending and a laborer stopped beside him to observe some work.

"What the blankety blank are they trying to do down there?" he demanded, turning to the pastor. Then he noticed the business suit.

"Oh, blazes," he muttered. "You wouldn't know." And he walked away.

Borders chuckles and nods. "He was absolutely right," he recalls. "I hadn't the foggiest notion what they were doing."

As soon as the contractor was able to give approximate schedules for occupancy of certain buildings, Borders commenced an intensive campaign to obtain tenants. The FHA had insisted that the corporation set aside a rather large amount of money for this purpose. That money was never touched.

When able to get in touch with former residents of the area, these people were advised by letter, telephone, and personal visit that apartments were available in the Wheat Street Garden Homes. Then, both from the church pulpit and on his weekly radio broadcast, Borders announced that the Wheat Street Garden Homes were taking applications for apartments. After the second broadcast, no further mention was made of the apartments, since the application list was already more than three times the number of apartments available.

The apartments have two bedrooms, living room, kitchen, and bath, with front and back porch. Electric refrigerators and gas stoves are provided. Apartments on the upper level rent for $69.50 a month, and on the lower level for $72.50.

On May 26, 1964, as the first one hundred families moved into the development, a dedication service was held.

Not a large percentage of the former area residents returned. Many had found new homes and neighborhoods to their liking. A few could not afford the rental, which was prescribed by FHA regulations. Then there were some who simply had always lived in a slum dwelling and were either afraid to attempt to better their living conditions or had lost the incentive to try. And others had families too large to meet FHA specifications for rental of two-bedroom apartments.

The Wheat Street Garden Homes drew their tenants from three major areas of the city's populace. The largest group was those families who lived in the far outlying districts, and who wanted housing closer to their central city employment. The next largest group were those who lived in adjacent slum dwellings and wished to improve their situation. The third group were those families occupying apartments in federal housing projects whose income level now exceeded the ceiling for such dwellings, forcing them to seek housing more suited to their means.

Among the first one hundred families there were two white families.

As the Wheat Street Garden Homes became occupied, a marked effect was noted among the church's members. Persons in the congregation who themselves lived in submarginal homes, beneath the standards of the garden apartments, were heard to say with pride: "I had a part in those apartments. They belong to our church."

To date, the church has invested $191,000 in the housing project. Most of this was spent for preliminary planning and preparation of materials for the Atlanta Housing Authority. There were some fees to be paid for the loan itself. There have also been some additional interest charges, as the contractor was late in delivering the last of the apartments of this first unit. Although this is fully covered by the bonding company, the church has not yet taken the matter to court for settlement, preferring to wait until the second part of the project is completed and a final FHA accounting can be made. Much of the church's expenses will be paid back by the housing corporation at a later date.

The Wheat Street Garden Homes are controlled by a separate corporation, Church Homes, Inc. The twenty-member board of directors meets monthly, when reports are heard from the secretary, the business manager, and the superintendent of the buildings and grounds. A look at the corporation minutes reads like a family discussion. Decisions are made about spraying for roaches, the care of grass, painting of the buildings, erecting cyclone fences to enclose the playground area better, to name a few continuing problems.

Such matters as unnecessary noise are handled by registered letter. The tenant is warned that such activities will not be tolerated. As a general rule, the warnings suffice.

The board of directors emphasizes prompt payment of bills, not only the rent but other bills as well. There are constant reminders to the tenants on this point, and several classes on planning and managing family budgets are conducted each year in the church's Christian Education Building.

A central laundry facility is provided, and again failure to adhere to rules brings prompt warning.

For the most part, however, the tenants seem as desirous as the board of directors to keep the apartments a showplace in Atlanta.

Serving on the board of directors of Church Homes, Inc., has been a marvelous learning experience for many of the church members. They do not always agree, sometimes they do not all understand the problem, but they are encouraged to participate, to think, and to work together. One of the more remarkable qualities of this board is a willingness to assume responsibility for extra tasks, and to perform those tasks. No board member is paid.

Borders says: "In only a short time this board will be able to run the Wheat Street Garden Homes without my personal supervision. I am essentially a preacher. I have learned a great deal about other areas, but I am not a housing expert. I put my mind to it as best I could, but as soon as I can relinquish my post on the board of directors of the housing corporation, I shall do so. We want to train leadership, and some of us who have been in leadership positions must step aside when capable replacements are developed."

In the late spring of 1966, the board of directors of the Wheat Street Garden Homes approved plans of the lawyer and architect for the second part of the church's housing development. Plans called for 114 garden-type apartments, and 144 apartments in two high-rise apartment buildings. The latter were especially designed for elderly couples.

However, before construction contracts could be let, the United States Congress passed a rent-subsidy program, as part of its enlarged federal housing law. In essence, the federal government would pay something better than half of the established rent for approved housing. The housing would be available only to low-income families whose living standards were to be improved.

As is often the case with pioneering-type projects, such as rent-subsidy housing, an immediate search was started to find the project ready to go which would be suitable for the pilot housing project. The Wheat Street Garden Homes were well known to the personnel of the FHA regional office in Atlanta, where their second 100 percent housing loan had been processed. Washington was notified that the second phase of the Wheat Street Gardens project fitted the needs of the pilot project for the rent-subsidy program. Some modifications were necessary, but the sponsor was established and had been approved and title to the land was clear. Just as the Wheat Street Garden Homes had been the first to handle a 100 percent loan under Section 221 D-3 of the 1961 FHA Housing Act, the Wheat Street Garden Homes would be among the first projects with rent-subsidy housing.

Under the revised program, the high-rise buildings were set aside, although eight acres remain for their erection later. The number of garden-type apartments was increased to 160 units, all containing three bedrooms.

Under this new program, families must be carefully selected

according to income (and several other criteria) and this screening must be done by the sponsor's staff. The permanent housing staff will include a full-time social worker and a recreational agent. Certain facilities, designed to speed up the rehabilitation of children and families, must be provided.

The rent-subsidy program means that the Wheat Street Garden Homes will provide housing for the low-income, the medium-income, and later (with the high-rise) upper-income families. It is thought by the planners that this mixing of families of differing incomes will prove beneficial both to the tenants and to the housing project.

Final approval by Washington of the revised plans came in about four months from the inception of the idea of the Wheat Street Garden Homes project Number 2 as rent-subsidized housing. Construction was to be started in the spring of 1967, with occupancy expected in the summer of 1968.

The crash nature of this project did cause a delay in the construction of the shopping center. However, building permits were granted in late fall of 1966; actual construction started in January, 1967, with occupancy anticipated for early summer, 1967. According to the Reverend Mr. Borders, the farm camp will have to wait until this latest phase of the housing project and shopping center is well under way.

Thompson is still vitally interested and involved with the completion of the Wheat Street Garden Homes, but in his new position at the Atlanta regional office of the FHA, he is also involved with another housing project being developed under Section 221 D-3 of the FHA title. On the west side of Atlanta, approximately six miles from the center of the city, Allen Temple African Methodist Episcopal Church is in the process of developing a five-hundred-unit housing project which it is hoped will be under construction during 1967.

After discussing these new not-for-profit housing projects for Atlanta, basically for the urban area's growing Negro population, Thompson commented: "I don't know of another area with so many housing projects of this type under Negro sponsorship. It is true that the FHA and the Urban League had jointly explored the possibility of a Negro institution becoming a sponsor under provisions of this law, but it was the Reverend William Holmes Borders and his Wheat Street Baptist Church who first took this idea beyond the discussion stage. They did something. What they did has brought hopes of escaping the slums to many of our people. More importantly, Negro leadership, which had been more inclined to talk than act, has had to reappraise its position. Wheat Street is positive proof that Negroes can assume responsibilities, that not only the federal government, but also the white business and political leaders of Atlanta, will help us when we decide to shoulder our share of the responsibility. Our people see this now, and they want leadership that takes its responsibility seriously."

Borders constantly receives letters and telephone calls from persons wanting to know how to start similar housing projects. His standard reply follows:

"There is an FHA office in almost every major city in America. Call on the representative of that office. If there is no FHA office in your city, then write or telephone the FHA office in Washington, D.C., or write to Robert C. Weaver, now Secretary of Housing and Urban Development. He will respond to your letter. Better yet, go to Washington, for it is just that important. It is absolutely not necessary to use a go-between to introduce or recommend you.

"I happen to be a Baptist, and we believe that it is not necessary for anyone to recommend us to God. We pray to God direct, ourselves. Now if man can go directly to God, you can certainly go directly to another human being here on earth. So go ahead. Sit down with your nearest FHA representative and talk about housing. What happened to the Wheat Street Garden Homes can happen in your city. It can happen in your community. It can happen in your church. But it won't happen unless you personally do something about it."

12

After the Marches

THE VERY OBSERVANT EDITOR of the Atlanta *Constitution*, Ralph McGill, has described the growing misery of our city slums in this manner: "The slum problem is easy to oversimplify. This is dangerous because it is a complex, human condition. But in general, it is a situation in which a great many persons are absolutely helpless to cope with the facts of life and the environment in which they live. They are helpless to do so for many reasons, all related. Most of them are from the South's rural revolution."

The South's rural revolution, of which Editor McGill speaks, has been occurring as a migration from the farm to the city and dates back to World War I. It was this outmigration of unskilled farm laborers that had so shrunken the membership of the Swift Creek Baptist Church, many long years before, and contributed to the broken health and heartache of the preacher-father of the Reverend William Holmes Borders.

There has been little or no letup in this migration as the untrained, unskilled, or semiskilled have left the fields for the city in search of better jobs and an easier life. For most of these people, despite the years of full employment and high pay during World War II, they have but exchanged the hardships of the farm for the hardships of the city, for here the road of hope and escape has come to an abrupt end. Today there are second and third generations born in the slums who know no other life. In all probability they are destined to remain in the slums for lack of incentive, proper education, adequate job training, and sufficient job opportunities.

With these idle lives gnawing on wasted hopes and despairs, it took but minor incidents during the long hot summer nights to spark destructive riots in the Negro ghettos of many major American cities. Following the second flare-up in the race-torn Watts area of Los Angeles, John A. McCone, former director of the Central Intelligence Agency, who headed an investigation into the original Watts riots that claimed thirty-four lives in August, 1965, emphasized two points in his statements to the press:

"If you recall our report, we said a contributing cause was the continuing exhortation of some leaders of the civil rights movement for extreme action to correct real or imagined wrongs.

"Unless the Negro people are resolved to help themselves, no amount of action can help."

The human helplessness found in our urban slums, as defined by Editor McGill, and the development from within the slum of responsible leadership and incentive, as defined by McCone, are not necessarily contradictions. The case of Borders and other responsible Negro leaders around the country is proof that out of the slums can come educated, trained leadership, dedicated more to the good of their people than to lining their own pocketbooks. But such leadership cannot be legislated into being, or advertised for in help-wanted classified columns of the newspaper. It must already be there, quietly at work. It must have established communications across racial lines; it must have access to white leadership willing to help the Negro meet the problems of his people, rather than solve the white leadership's vote problem.

However, white support for the emergent Negro leadership does not mean the subservience of that leadership to the pressures of the white community when such pressures run counter to the rights and needs of the Negro community.

Now many white people in Atlanta had acted like white people in other American cities. They dismissed from mind the unsightly problems of the Negro slum by either moving to the suburbs or avoiding the slums. If a problem isn't seen, it is more easily forgotten. But civil rights could not so easily be dismissed, for the issue repeatedly made front-page news in major daily newspapers across the country, Atlanta not excepted.

To present a balanced picture of Negro leadership in Atlanta, the local newspapers had done an excellent job of publicizing the Wheat Street Baptist Church's housing project. Undoubtedly some people remembered the pastor's name from previous stories. Is this the same Borders who integrated the buses without riots or problems? Good man! Glad we have him! And there for some the thinking stopped.

Thus, when it became known that Borders was involved with the student street marchers seeking to desegregate the restaurants of Atlanta, there were some white people who felt strangely let down. A few were angry and telephoned or wrote to him demanding an explanation. He gave that explanation in his next radio talk.

He explained that he was chairman of the Adult Liaison

Committee for the Student Non-Violent League. The committee's function was to support, and in measure to help direct, the student marchers. The committee would raise the necessary funds to support the marchers. The committee had met with city officials, and with officials of the Atlanta Hotel and Restaurant Association. He pointed out that most of the association members did not oppose integrating their facilities. The marchers were demonstrating against the few who did oppose their demand for fair and equal treatment under the Constitution and the decisions of the courts.

"Yes, I am for the sit-ins, the marching," he said. "There is a time when the good they perform cannot be accomplished by other means. But I do not believe that civil rights goals are attained only through marching, sit-ins, wade-ins, and kneel-ins. God bless the marchers! God bless their accomplishments, their sincerity, and the good they have and will accomplish.

"However, I sincerely believe that there must also be a local productivity. By productivity I mean constructive action which clearly demonstrates the Negro can and will take his share of responsibility. If we are to be ready for all the privileges of the Constitution, which we are supposed to have, which our civil rights movement, yes, with its marches and the sit-ins, are winning for us, then we cannot escape our responsibility also to perform in the spirit of that Constitution.

"I believe in demonstrating the wrongs done to the Negro. I also believe the Negro must demonstrate his ability to perform responsibly.

"I believe the preacher should lead his people. The preacher should help demonstrate how the Negro has been wronged; and the preacher should be in the forefront to demonstrate how his people are ready and willing to shoulder additional responsibilities.

"I have been active in civil rights, have supported civil

rights all my life. I have viewed civil rights with these twin goals in mind: demonstrate the wrong and demonstrate that you can handle the right. Nothing has happened which has changed my belief that responsibility goes with rights. It has been so since Adam, the first man. It remains unchanged in God's laws today."

There was an interesting personal sidelight to these marches.

"It was nearly ten years since my wife and I had been in India, and had been inspired and awed by the lofty principles and accomplishments of India's civil rights leader. Of course I could not impart his philosophy, his love of all men, to those eager and angry students in the short time available. I did try to whet their appetite to read more of Gandhi's writings. For myself, all during the days of the marches, I kept recalling Gandhi's statement, 'One day the black races will rise like the avenging Attila against their white oppressors, unless someone presents to them the weapons of satyagrahi [nonviolent resistance].'

"I prayed that we would truly learn to use nonviolence as had Gandhi."

A few months after the street marches, the Progressive National Baptist Convention of America met at the Wheat Street Baptist Church for their annual meeting. At the close of their week-long session, the convention unanimously passed a resolution praising the courteous and friendly treatment given their three thousand delegates in the various hotels and eating establishments of Atlanta.

However, it had been the marches, not the resolution, which had made the newspapers around the country.

In the early spring of 1966, Borders was appointed chairman of the Education Committee of the Summit Conference, the conference representing six of the major civil rights groups at work in the Atlanta area. The purpose of the committee was to formulate a program of action to ensure that Negro children would have educational opportunities and advantages equal to those of the white children in Atlanta, and to make sure that the United States Supreme Court decision desegregating the public school system was being carried out in Atlanta.

Three days later he was appointed to the city-wide Education Commission, whose primary duty was to present to the people of Atlanta the reasons why a proposed public school bond issue of more than twenty million dollars should be passed.

"I am glad to serve," Borders said upon accepting this call. "I believe that education is perhaps the greatest single need of the Negro people. If I wasn't a preacher, I'd probably say education was our number one need. But there can no longer be doubt that if we are to be led out of the slums, it will not be by marching but through the power of education to train and prepare our people for the advanced technological society we are now entering. As a Negro, I am glad to serve on this committee, and as a committee member I shall seek to serve the needs of the entire city.

"Our educational dropouts are a disgrace, a disgrace to the entire community. The community cannot afford dropouts. In another ten years a person who does not have a good education, who is untrained, will not have a ghost of a chance. He will have to live by begging, or handouts, or stealing, or charity. Better that we spend the necessary money now to educate than for society to support this unproductive dropout later. We need education. I am pleased to serve."

The bond issue promised to eliminate double classroom sessions, which now exist primarily in those schools located in the crowded Negro areas of Atlanta. To accomplish this the bond issue proposed to build additional high schools and elementary schools in these crowded Negro districts.

More than 80 percent of the total bond issue will be spent for new and improved educational facilities in the Negro areas. Yet there were some Negro leaders and followers who feel that to build public schools in the Negro areas would retard integration in the Atlanta public school system. These Negroes opposed the bond issue.

"This contention simply is not true," Borders said in one of his first public speeches for passage of the bond issue. "We must build the schools where the people are. It is not the business of the Board of Education to attempt to shift the population. This is not the Board of Education's problem. The problem, and the sole problem, of the Board of Education is to educate children. You can't educate the children where the children aren't. It doesn't make sense.

"Now if the white people run from the Negroes when we move into the same area, then they'll just have to run. God bless them. They have no right to run, for where will you go to get away from a person who has just as much right to be on this earth as you? Let them run, I say. That isn't our problem, either.

"Our problem is to devote our time and our energy, and the resources made available to us through this bond issue, to develop the greatest school system on earth. If we develop such a school system, the white folks will run back to that school to get the information and the training it offers.

"Now I am quite serious about this. People didn't run away from George Washington Carver, they ran to him. White people didn't run away from Booker T. Washington, or W. E. B. Du Bois, now did they? And they flocked to the ring to see Joe Louis fight, didn't they? Now, if down in your subconscious mind you want to stop white people from running from the Negro, then we must produce the best within ourselves.

"Education is a rock-bottom basic need. Not until we have achieved an education that commands respect will the Negro leave the slum. It is not enough that a few of our leaders become highly educated, respected and useful leaders in society. We want all Negroes to earn a good living, to have decent homes, to be respected. To do that we must educate the masses. The bond issue is a step in that right direction."

In the spring of 1966, the school-bond issue passed by a sizable majority, and in some of the Negro precincts by as much as four and six to one.

For one so active in the affairs of his people, and therefore well acquainted with the machinery of politics at city, county, state, and federal levels, it was inevitable that Borders would become a candidate for political office. In 1965 he ran for the Georgia State House of Representatives as a Republican, because "I think the South needs a two-party system." The decision to enter the race was made late. Almost simultaneously with the public announcement of his candidacy he learned that his wife was dying of cancer. He refused the suggestion that he withdraw from the race. "We will still have a two-party system," he said, "even if one party has lost his heart."

The election was lost by 10,000 votes, and three months later he buried his beloved wife, Julia Pate Borders.

Just before she died she wanted to know why it had to be now, just when there were signs of hope for the Negro, just when life was becoming most exciting.

"I couldn't answer her," he said quietly, "only God can answer that question."

One evening when he was sitting with her at the hospital,

she had reached over and taken his hand. "Holmes," she said, "promise me that you will go right on fighting for the rights of our people. You know, Holmes, Odysseus kept right on sailing in search of that port called home. So keep on sailing, Holmes, keep on fighting for our people, until the Master calls you home."

At the present moment Borders has no active political plans, although he says, "If I think my running will benefit the people, I would not hesitate a minute to announce my candidacy again. And this time I'll campaign."

He says this despite the fact that many people protested his candidacy on the ground that a minister had no business seeking political office. Some people felt it was not the proper life and association for a minister, and others felt that the preacher belonged in the pulpit, period.

"So much of our life today is political," he says, "that the preacher is involved in politics by necessity, if not by choice. Jobs are political, jobs from dogcatcher to that of President of the United States. Street lights are political. The church simply cannot escape politics, nor should it."

This realization came one day when he sat down and started a list of church activities which involved some form of politics or political contact, or license, or charter, or government inspection. Dealing with just the credit union, nursery school, and housing project, the list grew and grew and still was incomplete. Then he sought to compute the amount of personal time that politics took from his working day each week of the year. "I was staggered," he recalls, "I was working for the political government and didn't know it."

This, he realized, had been going on ever since he became interested in voter registration. He had encouraged voter registration from his church pulpit and in his radio broadcasts, and had taken voters to the polls in the church buses. He didn't try to evaluate his time spent establishing the nursery school, much less the housing project.

"I believe the pastor's first obligation is to God," Borders declares. "His next obligation is to the community and the people where he serves. If the preacher is going to protest actions in the political area and state publicly that these areas need improvement, then he had better personally seek to improve them. Now we have some tremendous statesmen and leaders in Georgia, but overall, I have thought some improvements could be made. I still think so."

13

A Long, Long Way

After the death of his wife, the Reverend William Holmes Borders moved into a small bedroom in the house that provides office space for the Wheat Street Church's credit union. It is directly behind the church, between the church and the Christian Education Building. "I wanted to be where the action is, to meet the people, to see the problems firsthand, and to pick up the fallen and get things done. There must be a purpose to living, and when there is a purpose, you keep busy."

He no longer found that purpose in the big house he had shared with his beloved wife, so he gave the home to his daughter.

"When I went to that home where we were privileged to live," he said, "it was of her making. All of the color schemes of the different rooms, the furniture arrangements, the rugs, curtains, all were here. I stayed in that house fifteen minutes and I could not stand it. The material house was there, but without my wife and without her spirit I did not want the house. I am glad my daughter can enjoy it, but even now, I do not linger too long in that house. It was made into a home by her for me, and without her it has a sadness that I cannot stand."

Certainly the problems brought to the new church study, which go far beyond his toil as pastor of Wheat Street Baptist Church, are challenging enough to keep him busy.

Not long ago several members of the Home Mission Board of a large white denomination called on Borders. Their problem was typical of the urban city area, for despite much talk of ecumenical action among the Protestant denominations—with an ultimate goal of the brotherhood of Christians in one church, one faith—there still exists the old racial barrier.

A church of this denomination, a sizable church with an education building, modern and fully equipped, was in financial trouble. Negroes had moved into the neighborhood and most of the white congregation had moved away. The church was unable to meet expenses with the handful of white parishioners who remained, most of whom were pensioners and unable to move.

The Home Mission Board members wanted to know if Borders knew of a Negro pastor, well trained and responsible, who might be interested in taking over this church at little more than the remaining balance of the mortgage.

Borders did know of such a pastor and introductions were made. The Negro clergyman was questioned at length on his attitude toward white people and his willingness to permit the remaining handful of white members to continue worship in this church if they wished to do so after Negroes were admitted to the congregation.

Borders made no comment, but his secretary repeated one

of his oft-stated phrases, "Whites will pay a high price for their prejudices."

Plans are for the white pastor to be called to another church. The denomination will quietly arrange for the Negro pastor to take over the pulpit, to invite the Negro residents of the neighborhood to attend this church and to organize a responsible lay organization. Once this is done, the denomination will transfer the mortgage and contract sale to the Negro church body.

The Negro pastor of this former white church has the highest praise for Borders. "He has exhibited great faith and interest in me, which I appreciate. His contacts are so much wider, more diverse, than mine, or those of any other local preacher whom I know. Certainly, the Reverend Borders is our most dynamic local preacher. He seems to specialize in building up the community and all the people in it. He has been an inspiration and constant help to our local Ministers Conference here in Atlanta. He has so much creative energy, so much leadership and industriousness, that he simply is an inspiration to all of us as he fights for democracy and the church."

Dr. Gardner C. Taylor, newly elected president of the Progressive National Baptist Convention, has stated that today "the Negro is prodding, irritating, and driving this country toward the democracy it claimed nearly two hundred years ago."

The statement brings to mind the lines of Borders' poem, "Little William," where the Negro preacher speaks to God in prayer:

> Life is hard—deep waters, wide chasms and high mountains;
> I don't ask you to move the mountains, but give me strength to climb the rough side.

Today these Negro leaders are confident that the future belongs to the persons who have the vision to see that there is no way for the nation, the state, or the municipality to prosper with one side of its body politic paralyzed.

Borders points out: "The cities in this nation that have interracial goodwill and understanding, the cities that are trying to treat all of their citizens right, are the cities that are booming and prospering and going forward. God bless them. Their future is tremendous. Memphis, Tennessee, Atlanta, Georgia, and Charlotte, North Carolina, are examples. They are far from perfect, but they are closer to an advanced understanding, a human understanding of the problem of democracy for all citizens, than some others. With all my heart and in humble kindness I recommend goodwill in the hearts of all the people, across racial lines, on behalf of their brothers and sisters.

"There is no way in the world for the state of Georgia to prosper indefinitely with one third of its population, almost a million people, enjoying but three percent of the prosperity. The backbone of such a state economy is already broken before you come up to bat. But when you make opportunities, and provide jobs to all according to ability, to the same extent you accelerate the economy, you cause it to flourish and there is money, there is more of everything, goodwill, understanding, love of our fellow man.

"All problems can be solved with greater ease when communications across racial lines are kept open and there is a willingness for fair play. Not only does such an attitude prosper on earth, it causes God to smile in heaven, and makes the angels sing."

Constantly with Borders there is an emphasis on keeping channels open across racial lines. If someone mentions the name of a person, described as influential in a certain area of government, business, education, communication, Borders writes down that name. He makes all the inquiries he can about the person. In intelligence circles one would say he compiled a dossier on that individual's background, actions, areas of influence. Having informed himself to the best of his ability on this individual's political and business life, Borders does not wait for that individual to meet him, he goes out to meet the individual. Sometimes he makes an appointment and sometimes he doesn't. Sometimes he has a specific need and sometimes he doesn't.

"I do not want to waste the man's valuable time," he says, "but I want to create a fellowship between us. I want to point out our areas of common agreement and interest and to quickly explore our areas of disagreement. I am not argumentative. I want to establish fellowship. It may be a month, it may be a year, it may be longer. But if he is an influential person, and I am actively working for my people, it is inescapable that our paths will again meet. I want that next meeting to start out as a meeting between friends, where mutual understanding has already been established.

"Let me emphasize that once you start this, you enjoy it. I schooled myself to meet those persons who I thought could help my people. Once I had done so, I so enjoyed meeting strangers, people from another avenue of life, that I often introduce myself to complete strangers every place I go. This really is an enjoyable game, for you not only meet some lovely people, but you also meet some scalawags and vagabonds. Sometimes you find these latter persons have a remarkable understanding of spiritual values and God's eternal truths. Perhaps they have learned these values from a different set of circumstances, but it is refreshing to find out that our Lord reaches into the lives of all. As his handyman, I also seek to reach into all avenues of life.

"What I'm saying is that the person who strives to help his people must make it a point to open lines of communication to important persons in the community, but he must never overlook that he wants and needs to meet people from all walks of life if he is even to start to understand the basic needs of his people."

Today Borders has a fourteen- or fifteen-hour workday, as he keeps personal channels open to the members of the church, as he supervises the various present activities of the church. However, he also manages to find time to work on the new projects for the church, projects which seem uppermost in his mind.

One of these is the purchase of another farm. At least once a week he meets with Ben Hurt, real estate agent and member of the Wheat Street Baptist Church. Hurt found the original farm site, which the church was forced to sell. The preacher has Hurt scouring nearby counties, looking for another farm to buy.

He has placed the same restrictions on the purchase of the new farm for much the same reasons. "As a handyman of the Lord, I want to be certain I'm a good steward of the funds he has given me. This property must be so situated that we can expect area improvements to increase its worth. Of course prejudices might force us to sell again, but we are trying to check this situation out in advance a bit more carefully than we did previously. But we are going to have our farm soon. We need it now."

The preacher and Hurt have made several trips to look over farmland and one has the feeling they are nearing a decision.

The need for the land is twofold. The more pressing need has to do with the welfare of the children. The slums are more congested today than they were nearly ten years ago when this project was first tried. Off-street recreation is still limited.

"We've got to get our youngsters off the streets of a summer," the pastor states. "They need to see nature as God created it. They need to sit in the solitude of the woods in that majestic silence and think about God and themselves. They need to do constructive outdoor chores, like those found down on the farm.

"Some folks think I'm a little gone on this subject, but I quote them that statement of California Prison Warden James A. Johnson, who said, 'The finest prisoner is but a monument to neglected youth.' Some of those who complain the most about a farm camp are those who seek my help to control their son or daughter, whom they've permitted to run wild in the city. Yes, we'll have our farm for our kids, and soon."

The second reason for the farm is the supermarket. Already an entire block of small shops and buildings facing Auburn Avenue has been leveled and the land cleared, ready for construction. The church has invested about $140,000 in procuring this land and the architectural plans for the supermarket are progressing, although they must be held up until the housing project is farther along.

There will soon be 520 families in the Wheat Street Garden Homes, just across Auburn Avenue from the site of the shopping center. With more than five thousand members in the Wheat Street Baptist Church and with the area of the church and market site overcrowded with residents, it is likely that this venture will be profitable, especially since there are no comparable chain-store markets in the vicinity.

However, the pastor says emphatically: "Profit is not our major motive. Of course we must make a small profit to stay in business. But our major concern is to give practical training to our people in the conduct of business, an area where we are traditionally weak. We wish to teach, to train, to supervise, and to graduate young people trained in business practices until they can compete for jobs elsewhere on an equal basis."

The farm fits into the supermarket planning as a place where the church can raise its own cattle and hogs, have them slaughtered and dressed at a regular packinghouse and then sell the meat in its own store. The current high price of meat has caused much grumbling and diet substitution in the slum areas. "The meat we serve our tykes in the nursery school lunches, or which they get at our Sunday church dinners, is often the only meat they get all week. I am hopeful that through the savings we can realize by raising our own meat, these more destitute families will be able to put meat back on their diets."

Besides discussing architectural plans, studying the conformity of desired modifications to city building codes, considering basic service equipment needed, and so forth, Borders holds long conferences with young men, intelligent young men, although it is doubtful that any of them have held jobs for longer than three or four months at a time. Most were dropouts from high school. They have learned no trades. The preacher tells these men of his plans for the supermarket. He needles and challenges them to help him. He has started some of them restudying basic multiplication tables, reading about stock inventory systems, refrigerator systems, and so on. The training program is under way.

The preacher can tell you the cost of a Volkswagen panel truck equipped with a small refrigeration unit. It is his plan, since so many of the Wheat Street Baptist Church families are spread around the city as a result of the highway and housing programs, to serve these families on a regular basis with deliveries from the supermarket. The boys in training are pinpointing city maps to show where church families live and mapping out territories where they can solicit and deliver orders.

"We must train carefully," Borders says, "but these boys sense that we are going places. They are just commencing to drop that wall of social hostility and display a warmth and friendliness when we discuss our plans, our goals, their goals. They aren't ready to make such a switch yet, that they think of these as their goals. Everything is still the church's goal. But we are making progress."

Equipment for a self-service laundromat and dry-cleaning establishment is being investigated. A public bath is included in the plans. There are also plans to have a small bakery, a hardware store, and a beauty shop.

"We've got to have the best, the very best," says the preacher. "Off-street parking, front and back. Brilliantly lighted for nighttime shopping, a must with so many of our families having both parents working. And," he adds with a sigh, "God rest my poor daddy's soul, but it's going to be open on Sunday. With these people coming to the Wheat Street Church from all over the city, all of them a part of our fellowship, helping to pray for and finance this supermarket, they must be included in its services. Yes, the route boys can deliver their orders, but you know how women want to walk up and down the aisles and look at things for themselves. That big weekend family purchase they'll make themselves, and I've decided we'll give the ladies that opportunity. 'Course, I haven't heard from the Lord on this yet, and I'm still praying about it. But I think it is right.

"The members of the church are getting behind this project nicely. They know it is needed. And this knowledge is helping to make the farm project more palatable to those members who have bitter memories and fears of rural Georgia and the people who live there. Those who know the farm readily admit that we can raise our meat and sell for less in our supermarket. Also, we are farther along than we were before. I mean, we have more accomplishments, we are more confident of our individual abilities to achieve, to follow through successfully. This means a great deal."

The secretary comes in and whispers something in the preacher's ear. He shakes his head, but thinks better of it. "Send him in."

A middle-aged Negro man enters and loses no time getting right to the point. His brother had left home years before to go North to seek employment. This brother has never contributed anything to the care and support of their father, which burden has fallen on the speaker. Through all those years he alone has helped his father find ways to provide for his needs. His father had lived with them until his Social Security payments came and then the son found the father a room of his own. The speaker and his wife continue to look in on the father and help him. But now suddenly the long-missing brother has returned and moved right in with the father, living off the father's meager income.

"Your father has a little money set aside, doesn't he?" asks Borders. "The Social Security check is not his only means?"

"He don't have much, Preacher. My old man never made much."

"But he does have some?"

"Yes."

"The last time I called on your father," the preacher says, "he told me that neither you nor your wife had been to see him in over a month."

The man nods agreement. "We have four children, like you know. We're kept real busy. But we see my old man most every Sunday here at church and he can call us from the corner store if he needs something."

"Perhaps your brother provides your father with a sense of being needed, of being wanted, and offers companionship in a way which you, with your own family, cannot provide."

When his visitor does not respond, Borders quickly chooses his course of action.

"I'm going to tell you a story about myself and one of my older brothers. My mother worked as a seamstress to earn the money to send this brother to Tuskegee. He muffed the ball. He wasted his opportunity and failed at Tuskegee. He married and started work. He earned more money than my father, but he brought his wife to live at our house. When his firstborn arrived, the family could not find this brother of mine. He was simply delinquent and finally left his family. At times I hated that brother.

"I had just started preaching at this church and my father was living with me, when one morning a Western Union boy brought me a telegram. It was from my brother, saying he was arriving on the ten o'clock train. My daddy read that telegram and then he started watching me. I could feel my daddy's eyes following me around the room. I didn't know what to do. Finally, my daddy spoke. 'Holmes, what are you going to do?' 'I don't know yet, Daddy,' I said. 'When I know, I'll let you know.'

"Well, I went to the station and stood at the head of the train platform waiting. At first I thought my brother wasn't on that train, for I didn't see him. Then I saw a very ragged figure of a man, alone, weary, pride rubbed off, climb down from one of the last cars. I could hardly believe the change.

"This was my brother! I had a tendency to run. I had a new church. I had a reputation to make. I was ashamed of my brother. I didn't want him sponging off me and my family as he had sponged off my daddy's family.

"But my legs just wouldn't take me away from my brother.

I knew that I should practice what I preached. 'If a man say, I love God, and hateth his brother, he is a liar: for he that loveth not his brother whom he hath seen, how can he love God whom he hath not seen?' *

"I took this scarecrow of a man, my brother, home with me. This brother was ready to confess his wrongs, to seek my daddy's forgiveness. The realization that this son had turned from his evil ways and had thrown what was left of his life upon the tender mercies of our Lord was a blessing to my father that not one of his other children could have provided.

"Now I imagine you and your brother really have not had a chance to sit down and talk. I'd suggest you invite both your father and your brother to dinner at your house. Get acquainted. He is your brother, your wife's brother-in-law, your children's uncle. After you have talked, I want you to come see me again, but bring your brother with you."

The man leaves. Apparently this was not the answer he wanted.

The preacher shook his head. "The prodigal son returns," he said. "We have so much of this in the slums. A boy sees no hope at home, so strikes out on his own. It's just as hard elsewhere, but he keeps trying. Finally, when the body is weak and weary and the cold cuts through his clothing, he comes home. He makes inquiries until he finds where the old folks are living and moves in. He's home. Among the other children there is resentment and jealousy, especially if a little money is involved. Members of families can be cruel to one another when money is involved."

The telephone was ringing. It was Attorney Lewis Cenker, the housing project attorney, telephoning from Pittsburgh.

* 1 John 4:20.

He had seen a type of construction in a federal housing project in the Steel City which he felt they should consider. He described it to the preacher. If Borders agreed, he should notify the architect and see Bob Thompson at FHA, where some supporting regulations would have to be checked.

The preacher already had an appointment with Thompson, who arrived on time. Together they studied the ground plot for the second half of the Wheat Street Garden Homes. They placed an architect's overlay on that plot. They were concerned with the location of the enlarged swimming pool and the new off-street parking lots. After studying the overlay, they walked to the housing project site and continued their deliberations.

Now that the school-bond issue has been passed, Borders is busy speaking to every possible gathering on the importance of education.

"I believe that Georgia should have the best education on earth. I believe that for every state, but I'm in Georgia. This is where I work, where I live, where I'm going to die. I think Atlanta should lead Georgia in this venture. I believe that we ought to tax ourselves to the tune of the necessary millions, however many, to give every child in Atlanta the best education on earth. I believe we ought to have an educational system so efficient and so remarkable that teachers would be glad to come from Pennsylvania, from Maine, from California, from New York, to be in our school system.

"We cannot have a democracy with a low level of intelligence. We must all realize that unless we raise our level of education to a comparable level with the other race, we will continue to come out second best in jobs, housing, and the fulfillment of our wants and needs. This is inevitable. It is absolutely true. Now, with this public school bond issue we have a golden opportunity to see that our children get that kind of education.

"And you parents. The school board can't make your kids study. The school board can't make them want to learn. That's the task of you parents. It starts at least as soon as these kids start learning their ABC's. Parents, tell your children, keep right on telling your children, how important it is for them to learn, to get the best education available. And parents, that doesn't mean you sit in front of the TV and yell at your kids to get their homework done. If you can't personally help them do their homework, turn off the TV and see that conditions are such that they have a chance to do that homework."

On the drive back from the meeting on education, Borders briefly discussed the thrill of the two honorary Doctor of Laws degrees conferred on him during the summer of 1966 by Atlanta University in Atlanta and Howard University in Washington, D.C. "These were not my first honorary degrees. The first honorary degrees were given because I was a preacher. These were given because I have done something as my brother's keeper. I like that. And I like the emphasis today on education. If I run for political office again, it is more apt to be on the issues of education than anything else. We are getting started in Atlanta, but all Georgia must start."

In this southeastern part of the nation there is an old bromide that goes the rounds: a hot sun and a slow mule made a preacher out of many a south Georgia farm boy.

One has the feeling this preacher's calling, as a boy of eight, was indeed a calling of the Lord.

As the Lord's handyman, Borders has indeed been active in a variety of fields as he sought to lead his people to the worship of God, not mammon. Prior to 1966, this former Georgia farm boy had been awarded an honorary degree in the humanities and three honorary degrees in the field of divinity. These awards recognize his achievements in pioneering the way for church sponsorship of public housing as another step in improving the present and future life of his people.

Back at the church—it was now ten thirty—Borders started preparation of his Easter sermon, several days hence. He took from the bookcase his little volume of poetry, *Thunderbolts*, containing poems on the great biblical events as Little William and other early Negro preachers might have described them.

He opened the volume to a poem, "Battle at Calvary." The author's introduction gives credit to Milton's *Paradise Lost* and *Paradise Regained*, and also states: "Most often the Negro preacher referred to Jesus as a man of war, a captain who never lost a battle, the general of an invisible army, a hero winning victories without a sword. Insofar as possible, the Negro preacher would marshal legions of angels and militaristic figures, the good and the bad, in conflict—readily understandable to his people."

Near the end of the poem he found the thesis for his sermon.

> The army of evil buried Jesus in the grave,
> Sealed the tomb, and rolled a huge stone against the door.
> But God's Truth, God's Mercy, God's Faith,
> God's Love and God's Goodness,
> Went down into the grave of the General of Their Army.
> On the third morning, Truth, Mercy, Faith, Love and Goodness,
> Called a prayer meeting in the bosom of the grave.
> His stick of spiritual dynamite ignited.
> The grave was blasted asunder.
> Death became frightened; in a frenzy of fear, Death hid.
> God Almighty was marching; planting His footsteps on the brow of Calvary.

Jesus staged the mightiest comeback of antiquity.
And said, "All power is in My hands."

The next Sunday at Wheat Street Baptist Church the choir and congregation would sing "Lift Him Up" and "Christ Is All," and the pastor would preach that all power, even over death, is in the hands of Jesus. Before the congregation leaves the sanctuary, hardly a soul present would not have murmured a silent prayer, "Thank you, Jesus—you've brought us a long, long way!"